THE FOOD OF
MALAYSIA

Authentic Recipes from the Crossroads of Asia

Recipes by the cooks of Bon Ton Restaurant, Kuala Lumpur
and Jonkers Restaurant, Malacca
Food photography by Luca Invernizzi Tettoni
Introduction and editing by Wendy Hutton

PERIPLUS
EDITIONS

Distributed in the Continental United States by The Crossing Press

Contents

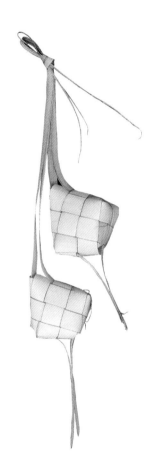

Part One: Food in Malaysia

*Where Asia's greatest cuisines
meet and mingle*

The Asian continent, encompassing the world's highest mountains, vast sandy deserts, millions of acres of fertile rice fields, massive river deltas and tangled jungles, comes to its end in the peninsula known poetically to the ancient Greeks as the Golden Khersonese.

This golden land, the Malay peninsula, lies where the monsoons meet and, over the centuries, saw sailing ships arriving from the west from Arabia, India and, much later on, from Europe. From the east came Chinese junks, Siamese vessels and the inter-island sailing craft of Buginese and Javanese from the Indonesian archipelago.

The original people of the peninsula—known collectively as Orang Asli and now numbering less than 100,000—consist of about twenty different tribes belonging to two distinct linguistic groups. Later arrivals, who spread south from Yunan in southern China and began settling in Malaysia around 4,000 years ago, were the ancestors of today's dominant group, the Malays.

The Malay kingdom of Malacca was the greatest port in the east during its heyday in the 15th century. By then, Malacca's sultan had embraced Islam, brought by Indian Muslim traders, and the new religion gradually spread throughout the peninsula. The lives of the Muslim Malays were to change during the 19th century when the British began, first in Penang, then in Malacca, to gain control over the Malay states. The British brought in huge numbers of Chinese and Indian workers, dramatically altering not only the ethnic and social structure of the country but its eating habits as well.

In 1963, the Federation of Malaysia was formed, with the states of the peninsula combining with the Borneo states of Sabah and Sarawak. Malaysia's cuisines are as varied as its people. The Malays, Chinese and Indians continue to create their traditional foods, while cross-cultural borrowing in the kitchen has led to a number of uniquely "Malaysian" dishes.

Then there is the food of the Straits–born Chinese, whose culture and cuisine combine Malay and Chinese elements. Their so-called Nonya cuisine is arguably the most creative and delicious to be found in the country.

The Eurasians, too—especially those of Portuguese origin in Malacca—have developed their own dishes, while the peoples of Malaysian Borneo add even more variety to the culinary scene.

Whatever their background, Malaysians love food, whether it's enjoyed at home with family and friends, eaten out at food stalls or restaurants, or is part of a festive celebration. We invite you to join the feast: *selamat makan!*

Page 2:
Viewing the coastline at sunset, it's easy to understand why the ancient Greeks called the Malay Peninsula "The Golden Khersonese."
Opposite:
The best of three major cultures—Malay, Chinese and Indian—combine with the food of many other ethnic groups to promise constant surprises.

A Land Where Nature Smiles

*Of fertile fields and teeming seas,
of dairies and durian orchards*

Malaysia seems to have been blessed by nature, which saves its volcanic erruptions, its typhoons and lashing monsoon rains and floods for other parts of Asia.

Covering both the tip of the Asian peninsula and the northwestern part of Borneo, Malaysia, not surprisingly, varies in terrain and climate. The "typical" lush tropical landscape— emerald green rice paddies, golden beaches fringed by groves of coconut palms—exists, but it is only part of the picture.

To the far north of the peninsula, near the Thai border, the climate is often dry and the landscape of endless paddy fields (for this is the "rice bowl" of Malaysia) relieved by abrupt limestone hills.

Much of the lush alluvial plain of the peninsula's west coast is planted with oil palm and rubber. This is ideal land for orchards too, and luscious tropical fruits such as the highly prized (and powerful smelling) durian, furry red rambutans, mangosteen, starfruit, *langsat* and other delights are grown here.

Rice fields, an indelible part of the Malaysian landscape, nestle at the base of Sabah's Mount Kinabalu, the highest peak in Southeast Asia.

Contrasting with this, high on the main mountain range, the Banjaran Titiwangsa, the temperate climate of the Cameron Highlands makes it perfect not only for holiday makers but for the tea plantations and market gardens which provide much of the fresh produce that reaches the peninsula's markets. Malaysians can thus vary typical tropical vegetables (such as water spinach or *kangkung*, bamboo shoot, eggplant, okra, sweet potato and taro yam) with temperate-climate vegetables like cabbage, carrots, broccoli and peppers.

The generally muddy coastal waters of the Malacca Straits on the west coast are ideal for crabs and shellfish, the mangrove swamps providing an important breeding ground for prawns and other marine life. The east coast, washed by the South China Sea, provides not only postcard-perfect beaches but ideal fishing grounds, and countless small *kampung* (villages) along the coast make their livelihood from the sea.

Some 300 miles or so across this sea lie Sarawak

PART ONE: FOOD IN MALAYSIA

and Sabah, characterized by traditional lifestyles and limited roads, especially in Sarawak, where rivers are still the major highways. Market produce is grown locally on a limited scale in Sarawak, where many inland peoples still rely largely on wild edible plants.

Although most of the populated areas of Sarawak are low lying, Sabah, by contrast, has a mountain range that culminates in Southeast Asia's tallest peak, Mount Kinabalu (13,455 feet). The local Dusun people living here grow "hill" (non-irrigated) rice, pineapples and bananas on the steep slopes of the Crocker Range, while dozens of market gardens around Kundasang (approximately 4,921 feet) grow a tremendous range of temperate–climate produce, including asparagus and mushrooms. Nearby, a dairy farm of contented Friesians produces a large percentage of the state's milk, while there is also a tea plantation.

A timeless Malaysian scene of fishing boats in an estuary, with simple thatch houses under the palms close by.

With such a variety of locally produced vegetables, fruits, seafood and poultry to choose from, Malaysians have few limits as to what they can create in the kitchen. The exception to this is that pork is forbidden to Muslims so it is never eaten by Malays and Indian Muslims.

A number of hotel restaurants, in deference to Muslim customers, substitute "turkey ham" or "beef bacon" for the real thing, and omit all pork dishes from their menu.

Seafood is very popular, and not just among the Malays and other coastal people. There is a superb array of fresh fish, shrimp, squid, crabs, lobsters and a variety of shellfish, not forgetting small dried anchovies, dried prawns and salted fish.

Most of the beef and mutton consumed locally is imported (often "on the hoof" so that it can be slaughtered according to Muslim dietary laws), while the Chinese raise pork, their favorite meat.

Each ethnic group in Malaysia has its own way of transforming nature's bounty, which can come slathered with spices or subtly simple, rich in coconut milk gravy or bathed in a piquant sauce. Malaysians are so varied that it is often difficult to make generalizations.

For example, everyone's staple food is rice. But then again, noodles are widely eaten at breakfast, lunch and dinner! Perhaps the only universal quality is Malaysian food's irresistible flavor, whether it is a stick of sizzling Malay satay, pungent Indian mutton soup, Nonya chicken curry fragrant with lime leaves, Chinese pepper crab or Eurasian saltfish and pineapple curry.

The Golden Khersonese

Malay food: coconuts and spice and all things nice

Nobody who has sat under the stars on a warm tropical night and smelled the tantalizing fragrance of satay—tiny spiced kebabs—sizzling over charcoal at a nearby food stall can resist Malay food.

For generations, the Malays lived a life relatively undisturbed by outside traders and invaders, apart from the heady days of the Malacca Sultanate. Dwelling along the coasts or river banks, the Malays enjoyed a largely peaceable existence, untroubled by the wars, famines and plagues that beset many other countries of the Asian continent.

Fish were abundant, rice grew in the paddies, wild and cultivated fruits and vegetables were available year-round in the constant climate. Fragrant herbs grew effortlessly, as did the indispensable coconut. Traditional meals were based on rice, with fish, vegetables and chili-based *sambals* to add extra zing.

Traveling along today's highways that cross the peninsula from north to south and east to west, it comes as a surprise to learn that until well into the 20th century, travel through what was a largely jungle-covered land was very limited. As a result, regional styles of cuisine developed in different parts of the Malay peninsula.

The northern states of Kedah, Perlis and Kelantan, all of which border on Thailand, and Trengganu, which rubs shoulders with Kelantan, show distinct Thai influences in their cuisine. So, too, does Penang. A tangy and fragrant sourness is often added by the use of tamarind, sour carambola and limes, while fiery hot chilies so often present in Thai food are also popular in the northern Malaysian states.

Fresh herbs often give a special touch to northern dishes. In addition to the herbs commonly used throughout Malaysia—lemongrass, *pandan* leaf, the fragrant leaf of the kaffir lime and the pungent polygonum or *daun kesum*—they include a type of basil popular in Thailand (*daun kemangi*), leaves of a number of rhizomes, such as turmeric and zedoary (known locally as *cekur*), and the wonderfully fragrant wild ginger bud.

A popular northern dish, Nasi Ulam or Kerabu,

consists of rice mixed with as many fresh herbs as can be found in the garden or market. A platter of fresh herbs or *ulam* is sometimes served with a spicy chili sauce, rice and other cooked dishes.

Settled largely by the Minangkabau people from West Sumatra, the central state of Negri Sembilan reflects its history in its food, with richly spiced dishes cooked in lashings of rich coconut milk, Rendang being a perfect example. The Malay cuisine of Johore, in the far south, includes a number of Javanese influences, as groups of Javanese settled here over the past couple of centuries.

Right:
Food stalls throughout the country are popular for inexpensive, home-cooked food. Nasi Campur (mixed rice) allows diners to pick and choose from a variety of cooked Malay-style dishes which are eaten with rice.
Opposite:
Local markets are filled with a bewildering variety of fresh and dried produce. The Central Market in the northeastern town of Kota Bahru is renowned for its wide variety of fresh herbs, often used to make Nasi Ulam or Kerabu.

Largely isolated from the rest of the peninsula until well into the 20th century, the state of Pahang, with its dramatic jungled mountains and gorgeous sandy beaches, offers a relatively simple cuisine, with fish from the ocean or the rivers predominating.

Other states of Peninsular Malaysia tend to be more multiracial in character, and the indigenous Malay food is less distinctive than that of other areas.

Despite regional differences, Malay food can be described as spicy and flavorful, although this does not necessarily mean chili-hot. But you can rest assure that even if the main dishes are not hot, there'll be a chili-based *sambal* on hand.

Traditional Southeast Asian spices have been joined over the centuries by Indian, Middle Eastern and Chinese spices, so the partnership of coriander and cumin (the basis of many Malay "curries") is joined by pepper, cardamom, star anise, and fenugreek—just to name a few of the many spices in the Malay cook's cupboard.

Food without seasoning is unthinkable—even a simple slice of fried fish is rubbed with turmeric powder and salt before cooking. Many of the seasonings that enhance Malay food are not dried spices but rhizomes, such as fresh turmeric and *lengkuas* (galangal), and other "wet" ingredients like chilies, onions and garlic.

Fresh seasonings and dried spices are normally pounded to a fine paste and cooked gently in oil before liquid—either creamy coconut milk or a sour broth—is added, together with the vegetables, meat or fish.

Food for the barbecue is also marinated or simmered in spices before cooking, and leftover rice will be turned into a tasty Nasi Goreng by first frying pounded onions and chilies.

With fish having always played such an important part in the Malay diet, it's not surprising that even today, tiny dried anchovies (*ikan bilis*) and dried shrimp are added to many dishes for flavor. And then there is dried shrimp paste or *belacan*, which, despite its pungent odor when raw and

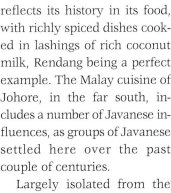
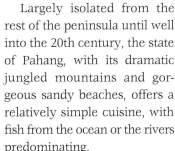

Right:
*Rice, the staple
food throughout
the country,
comes in many
different varieties
and colors,
ranging from
white to reddish
brown and black.*
Opposite:
*Malaysia's much-
loved cartoonist,
Lat, remembers
his childhood
(and food) in the
kampung.*

detached houses with minimal gardens. Modern lifestyles leave little time for gardening or preparing complex dishes, and a number of Malay dishes are now prepared mainly for special festivals or weddings.

The *kenduri* or feast is one time when Malay cuisine comes into its own. All the women of the family or village take out their giant cooking pots and work virtually through the night, scraping and squeezing coconuts for milk, pounding mountains of shallots, garlic, chilies and spices, cutting and chopping, simmering and stirring, until they have created an impressive array of fish curries, *gulais* (curries) of vegetables bathed in coconut milk and seasoned perhaps with fresh shrimp, coconut-rich *rendang* of beef or chicken, tingling

during cooking, gives an irresistible extra flavor to countless dishes.

The traditional *kampung* (village) house set in a cleanly swept yard shaded by coconuts, bananas and other fruit trees, with chickens pecking their way around a variety of kitchen herbs and vegetables, is increasingly something of the past.

Malaysia is modernizing rapidly, and more and more of its people are moving into terraced or semi-

hot shrimp sambals, and a colorful array of desserts.

With their innate courtesy and hospitality, the Malays consider it an honor to be able to invite any fortunate passerby to join in the *kenduri*. Women sit separately from the men, while babies crawl about or swing in a sarong cradle nearby. Children either peek shyly at the guest or race about happily—after, of course, enjoying the sumptuous feast that shows Malay cuisine at its best.

Celestial Cuisine in Nanyang

Chinese food: a two-way exchange of ingredients and culinary styles

Gas jets spurt like fire-breathing dragons, engulfing huge cast-iron woks where a mass of noodles is being tossed, seasoned and scooped by a perspiring Chinese chef. This scene is reenacted at food stalls and restaurants throughout Malaysia, where Chinese cuisine has become an inseparable part of the magical Malaysian mix.

When Chinese merchants sailed their junks across the South China Sea, visiting the ports of north Borneo before lengthy trading sessions in Malacca, they set in motion a process that was to have a profound influence on the region.

"Nanyang," the lands across the Great Southern Ocean, became renowned as a source of exotic ingredients and wealth. A few of these Chinese traders stayed on in the Malay peninsula, often marrying local women and forming the beginings of Peranakan or Straits-Chinese culture. However, it was not until the arrival of the British colonials in Singapore in 1819 that the stage was set for a huge wave of migration.

Thousands of Chinese workers poured into Singapore, and as tin was discovered in the Malay peninsula, many moved north to areas like Penang, Malacca, Kuala Lumpur and Taiping. Others headed straight for the gold mines and coal fields of Sarawak, or moved to British North Borneo (now Sabah) to work on the land. More came later to labor in rubber plantations that soon altered the landscape and economy of the country. The Chinese brought with them the cooking styles of their homeland, mostly the southern provinces of Guangdong and Fujian, introducing the indigenous people of the Malay peninsula and northern Borneo to a range of ingredients now used by every ethnic group in Malaysia today: noodles, bean sprouts, bean curd and soy sauce. Their technique of stir frying small portions of food in a little oil over very high heat in a conical frying pan or wok was also widely adopted. In turn, Malaysia's Chinese developed a penchant for spices and chilies. Any local Chinese coffee shop or restaurant will offer pickled green chilies or red chili *sambal* to enliven noodles and rice-based meals. The Chinese borrow

Opposite:
When wandering spirits get hungry, they can be downright malicious. Fortunately, they can be appeased with offerings of food, incense and street opera during the Feast of the Hungry Ghosts.
Left:
Eating is considered one of life's most pleasurable pastimes, especially by Malaysia's Chinese community.

curry leaves from the Indians, use English condiments such as Worcestershire and tomato sauce, and add Indian and Malay spices to the cooking pot.

Almost any self-respecting Chinese cook can whip up a tasty Malay-style chicken or fish curry, and most versions of Laksa (a spicy noodle soup) are prepared by the Chinese. They're not averse to enjoying a number of Indian dishes too, especially some of the pungent fish curries and Indian breads, such as *roti canai* and *murtabak*.

Chinese food is widely accepted as one of the world's greatest cuisines. One of its hallmarks is the ingenious use of ingredients—the Chinese cook's ability to transform "spare parts" into something that tastes like an exotic luxury is virtually legendary. The Chinese also place great importance on the contrast of colors, textures and flavors, both within a dish and the overall meal.

The light, clean, non-greasy food of the Cantonese, and the pungent, chili-hot cuisine of Sichuan are well known abroad, with northern cuisine from Peking also attracting a following. Although the dominant dialect group in Malaysia overall is Cantonese, there are large numbers of Hokkiens, Teochews, Hockchews from Foochow, Hakkas, Hainanese and Henghua, often concentrated in a particular town or region, each with its own style of cooking.

All this means that although Chinese cuisine in Malaysia seems somehow familiar, it's also full of delicious surprises. Like the fiery punch of crabs fried with black pepper, chilies, salted soy bean paste and curry leaves, or the creamy texture of fresh rice-flour noodles or *kway teow* fried with shrimp, egg and bean sprouts. Malaysian Chinese, who enjoy their food so enthusiastically that one might almost wonder if they live to eat rather than eat to live, dine out frequently, at roadside stalls and in simple open-fronted coffee shops as well as more formal restaurants.

As many visitors have noted, Malaysia's Chinese always seem to be eating. After a light breakfast (maybe Western-style toast or perhaps noodles or steamed tidbits known as *dim sum*), there's room for a mid-morning snack (an Indian curry puff or sweet Malay cake). Lunch could be any type of noodles or rice with Chinese, Malay or Indian side dishes. Dinner might be a formal Cantonese meal, a vast spread of seafood at a restaurant, a family meal of rice, soup, vegetables and meat or seafood, or even Western fast-food. And before bed, there's probably room for just one more bowl of noodles or perhaps some fried bananas. With so many good things to eat, who can possibly limit themselves to just three meals a day?

Spicy Soul Mates

Indian food: banana leaf curry and flying bread—
Malaysia's Indians make their mark

Visitors to Malaysia, noting the proliferation of Indian Muslim food stalls, of Indian restaurants advertizing "Banana Leaf Curry," and the universal popularity of the pancake-like Indian bread, *roti canai*, might be surprised to learn that the Indian community makes up around only 10 percent of the nation's population.

Indian cuisines—especially those from the south, where most of Malaysia's Indians originated—share some similarities with Malay cuisine in their generous use of spices and coconut, so it took little encouragement for Indian food to catch on. And it's not just the easy-to-love flavors of Indian food that make it widely popular; Malay Muslims can rest assure that Muslim dietary laws will be observed in Indian Muslim restaurants.

Like their Chinese counterparts, Indian traders have been recorded in the region for more than a thousand years, but it was only in the 19th century that they came to Malaya in large numbers.

Most were brought in as contract laborers to work on the rubber estates, where miniature Indian villages complete with temples, schools and toddy shops grew up. Others came to work on the railways or in setting up the telecommunications network, while many Indian Muslims opened restaurants, textile shops or small sundry shops.

Although Malaysia has small communities of Sikhs from the Punjab region in India and Malayalees from Kerala, in the southwest, the overwhelming majority are Tamils from the southeastern state of Tamil Nadu (once Madras). Indian vegetarian food is justifiably popular in Malaysia. Southern vegetarian dishes are cleverly spiced (a popular combination is brown mustard seeds, blackgram *dhal*, curry leaves and dried chilies), often combined with coconut milk or freshly grated coconut for extra flavor. Steamed bread (*idli*) and the finest, crispiest pancake imaginable (*dosay*) are made from ground blackgram *dhal* and rice.

Traditionally, Hindu vegetarian meals with a mound of rice, some *dhal*, several spicy vegetable dishes, a glass of thin spicy soup (*rasam*), hot sour

Watching the preparation of Roti Canai, a Malaysian adaptation of an Indian bread, is almost as good as eating it.

pickle and yogurt are served on the ultimate disposable plate: a square piece of freshly washed banana leaf. Indian Muslim restaurants offering more robust fare, with spicy dry mutton, crab curry, shrimp, fried fish and other dishes as well as vegetables caught up with the idea, offering a spread of such dishes served on a banana leaf. Today, many restaurants simply advertize "banana leaf curry," meaning, of course, you eat what's spread on the leaf rather than the leaf itself.

India's most spectacular contribution to the Malaysian culinary scene is the *roti canai* (literally "flattened bread"). This is an adaptation of *roti paratha*, traditionally made with a mixture of white and whole wheat flour. The Malaysian version combines pure white flour, ghee and—the secret touch—a little evaporated or condensed milk for an extra light dough, which is kneaded and rolled into balls and left to stand.

Then comes the dramatic part, as the ball of dough is punched flat and then grasped at the edge and swung around in ever increasing circles to make a paper-thin pancake. This is then flattened, shaped and fried golden brown in ghee. Some theatrical *roti* makers will even throw the cooked bread into the air with a flourish before chopping it, karate fashion, with the edge of the hands.

Finally, the *roti canai* arrives crisp and crunchy, with bowls of curry sauce or *dhal* that normally accompany it. If the dough is filled with chopped onion and minced mutton or chicken before being fried, the resulting stuffed pancake, known as *murtabak*, is a meal in itself.

Malaysia's Indian hawkers have created unique versions of several local dishes, preparing foods you'd never find in India. Indian Mee Goreng, for example, combines fresh yellow Chinese noodles, bean curd, bean sprouts and dried shrimp paste. Another noodle dish is the Indian version of Mee Siam (itself a Malay version of Thai-style noodles). And then there's Indian Rojak, vegetables and deep-fried fritters with a sweet sauce, totally different from the Malay and Nonya versions.

Indian curry puffs—pastry with a spicy potato filling—have been adopted enthusiastically by the Malays and Chinese, who create their own versions, sometimes adding pieces of cooked egg and chicken and creating a superb shortcrust pastry that is deep-fried to a melt-in-the-mouth texture.

Rich Indian mutton or lamb soup is a universal food-stall favorite, while Indian curries featuring chicken or fish are popular throughout Malaysia.

Right: Provision shops catering to Malaysia's southern Indians sell everything from betel nut to spices, garlands of jasmine to posters of the latest Tamil movie heart throb.
Opposite: Indians have used spices to flavor food for thousands of years; Ayurvedic or traditional medicine also makes use of an astonishing range of dried roots, spices and herbs.

Feasts from the Jungle

Borneo food: ingenious ways with the abundant resources of Borneo

Smoked wild boar stir fried with freshly cut bamboo shoots, braised fern tips plucked from the jungle, sweet juicy clams fried with a slathering of chilies and herbs and raw fish salad drenched with lime juice are just some of the delights that come out of the kitchens of Malaysian Borneo.

Sabah and Sarawak are peopled by a bewildering range of ethnic groups, each with their own culinary specialities. The influx of Chinese immigrants during the 19th and early 20th centuries led to the adoption of certain Chinese cooking styles, especially stir frying, with seasonings such as soy sauce now found in almost every kitchen.

More recently, since the formation of Malaysia in 1963, the arrival of Indians, Malays and Chinese from Peninsular Malaysia has further influenced local styles so that today, traditional Borneo dishes are generally found only in the longhouses and remote villages of the interior, or in isolated coastal settlements.

Naturally, the diet of people living along the estuaries and coastline is dominated by seafood, and as the majority of coastal people are Muslim, pork is never eaten. Inland folk, predominantly non-Muslim, enjoy whatever can be caught in the rivers or forest, such as wild pig, deer and other jungle game.

Rice, especially "hill" rice grown in non-irrigated fields, is the favorite staple, although in some areas, a starchy porridge made from the sago palm is still enjoyed on occasion. The semi-nomadic Penan of Sarawak are renowned for their regular harvesting of the sago palm, as are the Bisaya in southwest Sabah, while some hill tribes such as Sabah's Muruts make a similar porridge from tapioca roots.

In many remote regions, the people of Sabah and Sarawak have developed methods of preserving food, an essential art in the absence of refrigeration. Although smoking is common, another speciality involves packing chunks of raw pork or fish into a wide bamboo or a glazed jar with salt and cooked rice. The flavor of this delicacy, which is left for several months to cure, is, to say the least, challenging to the uninitiated.

Lengths of fresh bamboo—the ubiquitous utensil of the jungle—are also packed with raw rice or meat and placed near a fire to steam.

Although cooking styles vary, the general trend is for coastal cuisines to be more "Malay" in their use of spices and coconut milk. Interior cooks make use of the abundance of wild vegetables (including several types of edible fern), herbs and sour fruits. Dried fish, dried prawns and dried shrimp paste are popular seasonings throughout Sabah and Sarawak, as they are in Peninsular Malaysia.

Opposite:

Wild bamboos make a readily available cooking utensil in the jungle. Just fill with soaked sticky rice, roast over a fire and enjoy!

The Food of Love

Nonya cooking: a happy marriage of Chinese and Malay cuisines

Until about a decade ago, Malaysia's unique and arguably most delicious cuisine was in danger of disappearing. Fortunately for lovers of fine food, increasing consciousness of Malaysia's diverse heritage and a desire to preserve it seem to have saved the cuisine of the Nonyas. An increasing number of restaurants now feature Nonya cuisine, and the printing of Nonya recipes in books and magazines now means that enthusiastic cooks of any ethnic background can reproduce this cuisine at home.

The so-called Straits-born Chinese, descendants of early settlers in Penang and Malacca, combine elements of both Chinese and Malay culture, quite unlike the mass of Chinese migrants who arrived around the turn of this century and up until the 1930s. These pioneering Chinese traders, many of whom became wealthy men, took Malay wives, although as time went on, children of these early mixed marriages generally married pure Chinese or the children of other Straits Chinese, thus greatly diluting any Malay blood they may have had.

The women, known as Nonyas, and the men, Babas, generally spoke a mixture of Malay and Chinese dialect, dressed in modified Malay style, and combined the best of both cuisines in the kitchen.

Typical Chinese ingredients (such as bean curd, soy sauce, preserved soy beans, black prawn paste, sesame seeds, dried mushrooms and dried lily buds) blended beautifully with Malay herbs, spices and fragrant roots. Being non-Muslim, the Straits Chinese cooked pork dishes Malay style, and added distinctive local ingredients (coconut milk, spices and sour tamarind juice) to basic Chinese recipes. The Nonya pork satay, served with a spicy pineapple sauce, demonstrates perfectly this felicitous blending of styles.

Straits-Chinese or Nonya cuisine often requires painstaking effort, and in increasingly modern households, there is little time to spend preparing complex dishes for everyday meals. In old-style households, the Nonya wife devoted all her time to running the home and supervising the kitchen, assisted by a small army of servants—a luxury few modern Malaysian women can indulge in. Another reason leading to the near-demise of Nonya cuisine is that today, many Nonya girls marry non-Straits-born Chinese, and therefore tend to cook the kind of food their Cantonese or Hokkien husbands are familiar with.

Distinct differences evolved between the cuisine of the Penang Nonyas and that of Malacca. In Penang, geographically much closer to Thailand, the Nonyas developed a passion for sour food (using lots of lime and tamarind juice), fiery hot chilies, fragrant herbs and pungent black prawn paste.

Opposite: These Straits Chinese or Nonya ladies, enjoying a game of cards, typify the fusion of Malay and Chinese elements which makes this culture and its cuisine so fascinating.

carambola or *belimbing* fruits were all transformed in the kitchen. The back garden also yielded the herbs that make Nonya food so aromatic: the kaffir lime leaf, pungent polygonum or *laksa* leaf, the camphor-smelling leaf of the rhizome, zedoary (*cekur* or *kencur*), fresh turmeric leaves and fragrant *pandan*.

One of the most popular Nonya dishes among Malaysians of any background is *laksa*, a rice-noodle soup which blends Malay seasonings with Chinese noodles. The Malacca Nonya version is rich in coconut milk, its basic spice paste made from dried prawns, fresh turmeric, chilies, dried shrimp paste, lemongrass and galangal (*lengkuas*).

Just one look and whiff of its fragrance will mark a Penang Nonya Laksa, which uses almost all the spice paste ingredients of the Malacca version, then adds the fragrant bud of the wild pink ginger, *laksa* leaf, pungent black prawn paste, shredded pineapple and raw onion, and drenches the lot with a tamarind–sour gravy with no coconut milk added.

Nonya cakes are renowned for their richness and variety. Most are based on Malay recipes, using inexpensive and easily available freshly grated tapioca root, sweet potato, agar-agar, glutinous rice, palm sugar and coconut milk, with additional flavoring from the *pandan* leaf.

Little touches often transform an already delicious dish, such as the Malay favorite made with glutinous "black" rice, coconut milk, palm sugar and flavored with pandan. Nonya cooks usually add a few "dragon's eyes," dried longan fruits, for an elusive smoky flavor.

As any Nonya cook would confirm, it's the little things that mean a lot.

Malacca Nonyas prepare food that is generally rich in coconut milk and Malay spices (such as coriander and cumin), and usually add more sugar than their northern counterparts.

Many simple and—in the days when every Malaysian house had its own garden—easily available fruits and vegetables were prepared in imaginative ways by the Nonyas. Unripe jackfruit, the heart of the banana bud, sweet potato leaves and tiny sour

When East Meets West

*Eurasian food: a blending of styles,
decidedly on the spicy side*

What sort of food would you expect from a Christian cook living in Malaysia, whose ancestors were Portuguese, Malay, Javanese and Indian? To find the answer, head for Malacca, the historic town on Peninsular Malaysia's west coast, just 90 miles from the capital, Kuala Lumpur.

When the sultanate of Malacca fell to Portuguese invaders in 1511, the new rulers sought to establish control by encouraging Portuguese soldiers to marry local girls, and by bringing a number of Portuguese girls to marry local men.

Portuguese rule ended more than 350 years ago, yet in the so-called Portuguese Settlement of Malacca, families have names such as Da Silva, Dias and Sequeira, and many of the people speak Cristao, a Portuguese-based dialect.

The only things Portuguese about Malacca's Eurasian community today are the Catholic faith and the names, and many of the people living here are often a mixture of several different Asian races.

The children of cross-cultural marriages during the 19th and 20th centuries, where one parent was most commonly English or Dutch, blend into Malaysian society today, and there are no enclaves of these Eurasians such as the one in Malacca.

Naturally, the mixed heritage of Malaysia's Eurasians has produced a fascinating cuisine with many excellent dishes. Cooks of Portuguese descent are renowned for their generous spicing, particularly in such dishes as Devil Curry, an adaptation of Goanese Vindaloo where vinegar and chilies vie for attention.

Perhaps the most striking characteristic of Eurasian cooks is their readiness to borrow ingredients from many cultures. Malay herbs combine with a favorite Chinese cut, belly pork, Indian brown mustard, vinegar and a paste of freshly pounded chilies. English or Dutch-style dishes are transformed from innocuous stews to distinctly Eurasian dishes with the addition of a splash of oyster or soy sauce, a handful of spices, a few green chilies or sour tamarind juice.

With so many culinary traditions to choose from, it's not surprising that Malaysia's Eurasians have produced such a repertoire of unusual dishes.

Dancers, tracing their descent from the Portuguese who ruled Malacca during the 16th century, entertain in the so-called Portuguese Settlement.

Part Two: The Malaysian Kitchen

From the mortar and pestle to the food processor—
the kitchen modernizes while flavors remain traditional

You don't need a range of exotic implements to cook Malaysian food. Most of the utensils found in the average Western kitchen can be adapted, although there are several items which will make preparation and cooking a great deal easier.

First and foremost is something to grind or crush the *rempah* or spice paste, the mixture of seasonings such as chilies, shallots and spices used to season many dishes. The rhythmic thump, thump, thump of a granite **mortar and pestle** is a familiar sound throughout the country, yet it requires effort, time and expertise to produce a beautifully smooth *rempah*, and the proper type of mortar and pestle is difficult to find abroad.

Many modern Malaysian cooks use a small strong **blender**, **coffee grinder** or **food processor** to deal with large amounts of ingredients, although the faithful old *batu lesung* is still kept for simple grinding tasks. (See Cooking Methods for details on how to prepare *rempah*.)

A large, solid wooden **chopping board**—in Malaysia, a cross section cut from a tree trunk—is used for a multitude of tasks, together with a solid **cleaver** with a blade about 3-4 inches deep. Any Asian supplies store should stock this type of cleaver, which is far more effective at chopping up poultry, fish and crabs and mincing meat than a normal kitchen knife.

For all types of Malaysian cooking, particularly Chinese, a **wok** is essential. The shape of the conical wok (*kuali*) distributes the heat evenly, while its sloping sides ensure that when you're stir frying, food falls back into the pan and not out over the edge. It's also more practical for deep frying, requiring less oil, and allows the right amount of evaporation for many dishes which begin with lots of liquid and finish with a trace of very thick sauce.

Choose a heavy wok (it's safer as it's less likely to tip over) in cast iron or specially treated steel. It's now possible to get woks with a nonstick surface which can be scraped with metal frying "shovels," unlike delicate Teflon-covered surfaces. If you are using an electric stove, try to find a wok that has a flattened bottom, or failing that, use a special ring that holds the wok securely.

To season a new wok before using it, rub the inside with a cut onion, then heat a little oil and fry the onion gently for a few minutes. Tip out the oil, rinse thoroughly with hot water and wipe the wok

Pages 26–27:
A mouth-watering variety of fresh produce gives Malaysian cooks an endless array of options.
Opposite:
Traditional kitchens may look romantic, but most Malaysian cooks prefer today's modern westernized kitchens.
Left:
Mortar and pestle.

dry. Do not use abrasives and scourers on your wok; hot soapy water and a sponge should be sufficient.

A long-handled **frying spatula** for stir frying, as well as a circular **perforated ladle** for lifting out deep-fried food, are essential partners to your wok. While on the subject of woks, it should be noted that extremely high heat is needed when stir frying food. Many electric stoves cannot achieve the ideal heat, and Malaysian cooks—especially Chinese—insist on at least one gas fire, often with a double ring of gas jets. If you are using an old-style electric stove which will not reach a very high heat and which cannot be quickly reduced in temperature, you might consider investing in a gas-fired ring for using with your wok.

A claypot (left) and bamboo steamer (bottom right).

Although by no means essential, a **claypot** or earthenware *belanga* is an attractive addition to your pots and pans. The first time you use it, you might like to try the Malaysian trick of gently frying a grated coconut until it turns brown. Discard the coconut, wipe the pot with a cloth and store. These pots are designed to go directly over a flame, and can also be used in an oven.

Steaming is a popular method of cooking. Chinese cooks traditionally used a bamboo **steamer** with a woven cover, placed inside a wok where it sits a few inches above boiling water. Bamboo is an ideal material, as it absorbs any moisture that condenses on the cover.

If you are using a multi-tiered metal steamer (which many Malaysian cooks now do), put a kitchen towel under the lid to prevent moisture from dripping back onto the food.

Stores selling woks usually have perforated metal disks which sit above the water level inside a wok and can be used instead of a single-tiered steamer. You can put wrapped parcels of food directly on this, or, in the case of unwrapped food, on a plate set over the perforated disk. Cover the wok with a large domed lid and keep the water level topped up and at a gentle simmer during steaming.

An electric **rice cooker** is a great boon if you're eating rice fairly often. It's foolproof, producing dry fluffy rice every time, and also keeps rice warm for latecomers. Alternatively, use a heavy saucepan with a tight-fitting lid.

Fresh **banana leaves** are often used to wrap bundles of food for steaming or grilling, the leaf holding in the moisture and seasonings and adding its subtle flavor to the food. A layer of parchment (not waxed) paper and another layer of aluminum foil or, if you prefer, just the foil—will make an adequate substitute.

A few less common kitchen tools are used for special dishes, although a little imagination will always produce substitutes. The four-spouted cup for making lacy *roti jala* pancakes can be replaced by a plastic squeeze bottle; a heavy frying pan substitutes for the metal griddle or *tawa* used for Indian breads, and large ladles will do the task of special flat mesh baskets used to remove noodles from boiling water.

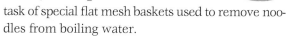

Cooking Methods

Mastering a few basic techniques
makes all the difference

Malaysian cooks use a wide range of cooking methods—pan frying and deep frying, stir frying, braising, boiling, steaming and grilling over charcoal or under a grill.

It's essential to know how to prepare the *rempah* or basic seasoning paste required for many dishes. Before beginning, all the ingredients should be finely chopped. The principle is to grind or blend the toughest ingredients first, adding softer and wetter ingredients towards the end. Whether using a mortar and pestle, a blender or food processor, the order is the same. First grind any dried spices or nuts until fine, then add hard ingredients, such as lemongrass, and galangal (already sliced or chopped in small pieces). Pound or process until fine, then add softer rhizomes, such as fresh turmeric and ginger, soaked dried chilies and sliced fresh chilies. When these are fine, add the ingredients that are full of moisture, such as chopped shallots and garlic, as well as soft shrimp paste.

If you are using a food processor or blender, you will probably need to add just a little liquid to keep the blades turning. If the *rempah* is to be fried, add a little of the specified amount of cooking oil, while if it is to be cooked in coconut milk, add some of this. While processing, you will probably need to stop the machine frequently to scrape down the sides. Continue until you have a fine paste.

Some cooks add water rather than the cooking medium to the blender; this means that the *rempah* will need to be cooked for a longer period of time before adding the other ingredients, to allow the water to evaporate and the *rempah* to eventually fry rather than just stew.

The spice paste is generally gently fried before any other liquid is added. Malaysian cooks will tell you to cook the *rempah* "until it smells fragrant" or "until the oil comes out," both accurate descriptions of what happens after 3–5 minutes of frying over gentle heat, stirring frequently. The spice paste must be thoroughly cooked at this stage or the resulting dish will have a raw taste to it.

Coconut milk is often added to the basic spice paste, generally in two stages. The thinner coconut milk is added, a little at a time, to the cooked spice paste, (often after pieces of meat or chicken have also been browned) and is stirred frequently, lifted with a ladle and poured back into the pan, until it comes to the boil. This process ensures the coconut milk does not curdle. The coconut gravy is then simmered gently, with the pan uncovered. The thick coconut milk or cream is added just before serving, heated through but not boiled, to enrich and thicken the gravy or sauce.

Page 2:
Verdant rice terraces sculpt the foothills of Bali.

Opposite:
Balinese meal of Sate Lilit (top), Yellow Rice, Urap and Grilled Chicken (right) and Black Rice Pudding with fresh rambutans (left).

Malaysian Ingredients

A cornucopia of basic items, ranging from the familiar to the frankly exotic

Asam Gelugur

Belimbing

Candlenuts

Most Malaysian ingredients will already be known to those familiar with Chinese, Malay and Indian food. These ingredients are described in the following pages, and a range of substitutes suggested. Where local names may be of help in identification, these are provided in brackets (M: Malay; C: Cantonese; T: Tamil; H: Hindi).

AGAR-AGAR: A gelatin made from seaweed which sets without refrigeration, used for cakes and desserts. Most Malaysian cooks prefer powdered agar-agar to strands. One teaspoon will set 1–1$^1/_2$ cups of liquid.

ANCHOVIES, DRIED: see **Ikan Bilis**

ASAM GELUGUR: Dried slices of a sour fruit (*Garcinia atnoviridis*) used instead of tamarind pulp in some Malay and Nonya dishes; the latter can be used as a substitute (see **Tamarind**).

BAMBOO SHOOTS: The fresh variety must be peeled, sliced and simmered in water for about 30 minutes. Boil canned bamboo shoots for 5 minutes to reduce any metallic flavor.

BEAN CURD: Several types of soy bean curd are used. **Hard bean curd squares** (C: *tau kwa*) have had much of the moisture squeezed out and hold their shape when fried. **Soft bean curd** (C: *tau foo*) is preferred for soups and for some dishes where it is almost "scrambled." **Dried, deep-fried bean curd** (C: *tau foo pok*), used in *laksa* and some other vegetable dishes, comes in small dark brown cubes which should be briefly blanched in boiling water to remove oil before adding to soups and stews. Sheets of dried **bean curd skin** (C: *tau foo juk*) are used as a wrapping, while strips of dried bean curd skin (C: *tau foo kee*) are added to meat and vegetable dishes. Small squares of **fermented bean curd** (C: *nam yee*), sold packed in jars, are used to flavor some Chinese dishes.

BEAN SPROUTS: Sprouted green mung peas are known locally as *tauge*. Sprouted soy beans are also found, although are less popular. Store in fridge covered with water for 2–3 days, changing water daily.

BELIMBING: Known by its Malay name locally, though sometimes referred to as carambola elsewhere, this pale green acidic fruit about 2–3 inches in length is added to curries, soups and pickles. The large, sweet, five-edged starfruit, is also known as *belimbing* or sometimes *belimbing manis*.

BLACK CHINESE VINEGAR: Made from fermented rice, this has a distinctive fragrance somewhat similar to balsamic vinegar and is used sparingly as a seasoning, and is traditionally added to sharksfin soup. Sometimes known as Tientsin vinegar.

BLACK SAUCE, SWEET: A thick, molasses-like sauce used in fresh spring rolls (*popiah*) and some other dishes (C: *tim cheong*).

BROWN MUSTARD SEED: A small reddish-brown seed used mainly in southern Indian cooking (M: *biji sawi*; T: *kardugoo*).

CANDLENUT: A round, cream-colored waxy nut (M: *buah keras*) pounded and added to Malay and Nonya dishes for flavor and texture. As they do not keep well, store in a jar in a freezer. As a substitute, use macadamia nuts or almonds.

CARDAMOM: The tiny black seeds of this intensely fragrant spice are encased in fibrous, straw-colored pods; smash the pod with a cleaver or a pestle before using whole. Decorticated cardamom seeds can be used as a substitute. (M: *buah pelaga*; T: *elakai*; H: *illaichi*).

CELERY: Local or "Chinese" celery (M: *daun saderi, daun sop*) is very different from the normal western variety, being much smaller with slender stems and particularly pungent leaves. Used as a herb in soups and some dishes. Substitute with the leaves of regular celery.

CHILI: Three main types of chili (M: *cabai, lada,* *cili*) are used: the normal finger-length **red** (ripe) or **green** (immature) **chili**; tiny fiery hot **bird's-eye chilies** (M: *cili padi*) and **dried red chilies** (M: *cili kering*). The latter must be broken in several pieces and soaked in warm water before being pounded. **Chili powder** (M: *serbuk cili*) is made from finely ground dried chilies; do not confuse it with American chili powder which is a blend of several seasonings as well as chili. **Chili oil**, available in small bottles, is used to enliven some Sichuan dishes.

CHIVES: "Chinese" or "coarse" chives, flat leaves about 12 inches long, are used as a vegetable and seasoning (C: *koo choy*). Because of their pronounced flavor, they are sometimes known as "garlic chives."

CINNAMON: The thick, fragrant brown bark of a type of cassia (M: *kayu manis*) is used rather than true cinnamon. The latter, a native of Sri Lanka, is much finer in texture and more delicate in flavor. Chunks of cassia bark, often used in meat and rice dishes, are preferable to powdered cinnamon.

CLOUD EAR FUNGUS: A shriveled greyish-brown fungus also known as wood fungus (C: *mok yee*), this should be soaked in warm water before use. The wrinkled, ear-like pieces swell to at least four times their dried size.

CLOVES: A dark brown nail-shaped spice always used whole and not in powdered form.

COCONUT MILK: In Malaysia, the grated flesh

Chinese Celery

Chilies

Coarse Chives

Cinnamon

Cloud Ear Fungus

Curry Leaf

Daun Kesum

Galangal

of the mature coconut is squeezed with water to obtain coconut milk. Normally, $\frac{1}{2}$ cup of water is added to 1 coconut and squeezed to obtain thick milk or coconut "cream"; the flesh is then kneaded with another $2\frac{1}{2}$ cups of water and squeezed to obtain thin coconut milk. The best substitutes are either powdered coconut (sometimes sold by the Malay name, *santan*) or canned unsweetened coconut cream, both of which should be diluted according to the manufacturer's instructions.

CORIANDER: Small beige-colored seeds (M: *ketumbar*) that are a vital ingredient in most spice mixtures. Fresh coriander leaf, sometimes known as **cilantro** or Chinese parsley abroad, is widely used as a garnish.

CUMIN: Frequently used in conjunction with coriander in curries, cumin (M: *jintan putih*) is somewhat similar to the caraway seed in appearance.

CURRY LEAF: An important ingredient in southern Indian cuisine and also used in some Malay fish curries, this small, dark green leaf (M: *daun kari*; T: *karuvapillai*) can be found dried in specialty stores abroad. No substitute.

DAUN KESUM: Sold under its Malay name, and sometimes also referred to as *daun laksa* (literally "*laksa* leaf") because it is traditionally added to that dish. This particularly pungent herb (*Polygonum hydropiper*) is sometimes known as Vietnamese mint, although it bears no resemblance to mint. In Japan, the peppery green is known as *akatade*.

FENNEL: An important curry spice, slightly fatter and whiter than cumin and with a sweet fragrance (M: *jintan manis*). This is sometimes mistakenly called anise in Malaysia.

FENUGREEK: Hard yellowish-brown seeds often used in fish curries and some Indian dishes (M: *halba*).

FIVE-SPICE POWDER: As the name implies, this is a mixture of spices (star anise, fennel, cloves, cinnamon and Sichuan pepper). Used in some Chinese dishes (C: *ng heong fun*).

GALANGAL: Known in Malaysia as *lengkuas* (*laos* in Indonesia), this ginger-like rhizome imparts a distinctive flavor to many dishes. Try to use young pinkish galangal as it is more tender. Always chop galangal before pounding or blending, as it is often tough. Slices of dried galangal must be soaked in boiling water for 20–30 minutes before use; a better substitute is the water-packed jars of sliced galangal exported from Thailand (where it is called *kha*).

GARLIC: An important seasoning in all Malaysian kitchens, the size of local garlic cloves is generally smaller than that of garlic sold in western countries. Use your own judgment in these recipes.

GINGER: Fresh ginger (M: *halia*) is used by all ethnic groups in Malaysia. Young ginger is pale in color with pink tips, and has much more juice than the mature rhizome. Scrape the skin off mature ginger with a knife before using. Do not substitute with powdered ginger, which has a completely different flavor; most supermarkets should stock this vital ingredient.

IKAN BILIS: Known locally by the Malay name, these small salted dried anchovies are used to season some dishes and are also fried to make a crunchy side dish or appetizer. Chinese stores sell a much smaller, thinner variety no more than 1 inch long, which has a slightly different flavor; this is sometimes sold as "silver fish."

JICAMA: Native to tropical America, this tuber with a beige skin and crisp white interior is also known as yam bean. Jicama (M: *bengkuang*) is frequently misnamed turnip in Malaysia.

KRUPUK: Dried wafers made from tapioca starch and prawns or fish; one Indonesian variety is made from a bitter nut, *melinjo* (*krupuk emping*). Make sure they are thoroughly dry before deep frying in oil for a few seconds, when they puff up spectacularly. Used as a garnish or snack.

LEMONGRASS: This fragrant lemony herb, which resembles a miniature leek, is used whole in soups or curries, or pounded as part of the basic spice mix. When pounding lemongrass (M: *serai*), slice off the root end and use only the tender bottom portion (about 4 inches); slice before pounding or blending. Dried or powdered lemongrass (often sold under the Indonesian name, *sereh*) can be

Lemongrass

used as a substitute. About 1 teaspoon powder equals 1 stalk of lemongrass.

LILY BUDS, DRIED: The Chinese aptly call these dried flowers "golden needles" (C: *khim chiam*). They are usually knotted for a neater appearance before being added to soups or vegetable dishes. No substitute.

LIME: Two types of lime are used in Malaysia. The larger lime is slightly smaller and less pointed than the average lemon, and changes from green to yellow when ripe (M: *limau nipis*). Slightly less acidic and more fragrant, the small round lime (M: *limau kesturi*) is sometimes known by its Filipino name, *calamansi*, abroad. Lemon juice can be substituted for large limes, while a mixture of lemon and orange juice (2 parts to 1) approximates the acidity and flavor of the smaller lime.

Limes

LIME LEAF, FRAGRANT: Also known as kaffir lime leaf and widely used in Thai cuisine, this adds an intense fragrance to some Malay and Nonya dishes (M: *daun limau purut*). The grated rind is sometimes used in cooking.

Lime Leaf

MUSHROOMS, DRIED BLACK: Dried mushrooms, either dark black or deep brown, should be soaked in warm water for 20 minutes before use, and the stems discarded. Varying in thickness and quality; buy the thickest and most expensive for dishes which feature mushrooms as the main ingredient.

NOODLES: Many types of fresh and dried

Dried Black Mushrooms

Palm Sugar

Pandan Leaf

Shallots

Dried Shrimp Paste

noodles are popular. Dried noodles include **wheat flour noodles** (C: *mien*), dried **rice vermicelli** (C: *meehoon*), and mung pea noodles (C: *sohoon*), known as **"cellophane"** or **transparent noodles**. The main types of fresh noodles are thick round **yellow noodles** made from wheat flour and egg; thin round or narrow flat **beige-colored noodles** made from wheat flour; wide, flat, white **rice-flour noodles** (C: *kway teow*), and round rice-flour noodles (*laksa* **noodles**).

NUTMEG: Used in some savory dishes and soups by Malay cooks. Try to buy the whole nut (M: *buah pala*) and grate just before using as the powdered spice quickly loses its fragrance.

OYSTER SAUCE: Frequently added to stir-fried vegetable dishes and meat, this sauce must be refrigerated after the bottle is opened. If you do not like monosodium glutamate, choose your brand carefully, as most are laden with this controversial additive.

PALM SUGAR: Generally sold in Malaysia as *gula melaka* (Malacca sugar), made from either the *aren* or coconut palm. It is available in hard golden-brown cylinders. Substitute with soft brown sugar and, if you have it, a touch of maple syrup.

PANDAN LEAF: see **Screwpine Leaf**

POLYGONUM: see **Daun Kesum**

PRAWNS, DRIED: Soak in warm water for about 5 minutes to soften before use, and dis-card any bits of hard shell. (M: *udang kering*; C: *hay bee*).

RICE: Many types of rice are used, the most popular for daily meals being fragrant long-grain white rice, with imported Thai rice preferred; some Indian recipes require the nutty flavored *basmati* rice, with a long, thin, faintly golden grain. Two types of glutinous or sweet rice are used in a number of sweet and savory dishes: the cloudy white grain (M: *beras pulut*) and the brownish-black grain (*pulut hitam*). All rice should be thoroughly washed in several changes of water before using.

RICE WINE: Used in Chinese cuisine; available in small bottles. Substitute dry sherry.

ROSE ESSENCE: A heady fragrance from the Middle East, used in Malay desserts, drinks and some Indian rice dishes.

SALTED CABBAGE: This should be soaked in several changes of water for about 1 hour to remove excess saltiness. Used in some Chinese and Nonya dishes (C: *ham choy*).

SALTED DUCK EGG: A popular accompaniment to rice and savory Malay dishes (M: *telor masin*). Wash off any black coating (often added to protect the egg), boil 10 minutes, then cut in half while still in the shell.

SALTED SOY BEANS: Usually sold in jars, with the soft fermented and salted soy beans in a brownish sauce (C: *tau cheong*). Mash slightly before using.

SCREWPINE (PANDAN) LEAF: Imparts a distinct yet subtle flavor to a range of Malay and Nonya dishes, both savory and sweet. The leaf (M: *daun pandan*) is either raked with the tines of a fork to release the fragrance and tied before being added to the pot, or pounded to extract the juice and add a touch of green color for desserts. Bottled essence can be substituted in desserts, but if fresh or dried *pandan* leaves are not available, omit from savory dishes.

SESAME OIL: Roasted sesame seeds are ground to make this oil, used only as a seasoning, not a frying medium, by Chinese cooks (C: *ma yau*).

SHALLOTS: Tiny round red onions (M: *bawang merah*), usually pounded as part of a basic seasoning mix or finely sliced and crisp fried in oil over moderate heat to provide a garnish.

SHRIMP PASTE: Shrimp paste varies in color and moisture content. **Dried shrimp paste** (M: *belacan*) varies in color and texture from purplish pink and rather moist to crumbly beige cakes or hard brownish-black squares. *Belacan* (pronounced "blachan"), which is sometimes sold overseas under the Indonesian name, *trasi*, must be cooked before eating; the easiest method is to wrap in a square of foil and grill or cook in a dry pan for a couple of minutes on each side, until dry and crumbly with a fragrant smell. *Belacan* must not be confused with the completely different **black shrimp paste** (M: *petis;* C: *hay koh*), a black molasses-like seasoning used by Nonya cooks.

SOY SAUCE: Two types are used in Malaysian cooking; **light soy sauce**, (M: *kicap soy masin*) which is thinner, lighter in color and saltier than **black soy sauce** (M: *kicap soya pekat*), which is generally used during long slow cooking or to give a dark coloring to a dish.

Spring Onion

SPRING ONION: Known also as scallion, green onion or most misleading, as shallot, the spring onion has slender stalks which are white at the base with dark green leaves (M: *daun bawang*).

Turmeric

TAMARIND: Dried tamarind fruits are generally sold in pulp form in Malaysia, with the stones and some other fibrous matter still intact (M: *asam*). The juice, used to give acidity and fragrance to many dishes, is obtained by soaking the pulp in warm water for about 5 minutes, then squeezing to extract the juice, which should be sieved before use. If using cleaned tamarind pulp without stones, halve the amounts specified in these recipes.

Wild Ginger Bud

TURMERIC: A rhizome similar to ginger in appearance but with vivid yellow interior. Fresh turmeric (M: *kunyit*) is generally preferred in Malaysia, although 1 teaspoon of powdered turmeric can be used as a substitute for about $\frac{1}{2}$ inch fresh turmeric.

WILD GINGER BUD: The pink waxy flower from a variety of ginger sometimes known as torch ginger (botanical name is *Etlingera elatior*). Used in bud form, it gives an inimitable flavor to some Malay and Nonya dishes. No substitute. (M: *bunga siantan* or *bunga kantan*).

Jicama

Part Three: The Recipes

Basic recipes for condiments, sauces and pickles precede those for main recipes, which begin on page 44

Malaysians generally present several dishes at each meal, allowing diners to serve themselves whatever they want. As a general rule, these recipes will serve 4–6 people as part of a meal with rice and 2–3 other dishes.

SAMBAL BELACAN

12 large red chilies, roughly chopped
2 tablespoons dried shrimp paste, roasted
$2/_3$ cup water
4 tablespoons lime juice

Blend the chilies and shrimp paste with the water. Season to taste with lime juice.

CUCUMBER AND PINEAPPLE SAMBAL

1 medium-sized cucumber, peeled, seeded and diced
$1/_2$ pineapple, peeled and diced
1 red chili, finely sliced
1 medium-sized red onion, peeled and sliced
$1/_2$ teaspoon salt
2 tablespoons sugar
3 tablespoons lime juice

Combine all ingredients in salad bowl and mix thoroughly.

Ingredients

When a recipe lists a hard-to-find or unusual ingredient, see pages 32 to 37 for possible substitutes. If a substitute is not listed, look for the ingredient in your local Asian food market, or check the mail-order listings on page 118 for possible sources.

Time Estimates

Time estimates are for preparation only (excluding cooking) and are based on the assumption that a food processor or blender will be used.

🕐 *quick and very easy to prepare*

🕐🕐 *relatively easy; less than 15 minutes to prepare*

🕐🕐🕐 *takes more than 15 minutes to prepare*

Opposite:
(counter-clockwise from top) Pickled Papaya, Stuffed Chili Pickle and Dried Cucumber Acar.

PICKLED PAPAYA

1 under-ripe papaya ($1\frac{1}{2}$ pounds)
6 tablespoons distilled white vinegar
3 tablespoons sugar
$\frac{1}{2}$ teaspoon salt
5 bird's-eye chilies, left whole

Peel the papaya, cut in half lengthwise and remove the seeds. Cut into very thin slices. Wash and dry the papaya. Bring the vinegar, sugar and salt to a boil. Remove from heat and allow to cool. Mix well with the chilies and papaya and keep overnight. Store in a covered container in the refrigerator up to 1 month.

Opposite:
*Mango Kerabu
(left) and
Cucumber &
Pineapple Sambal
(right).*

DRIED CUCUMBER ACAR

2 cucumbers ($1\frac{1}{2}$ pounds)
1 large carrot

Dressing:
$\frac{3}{4}$ cup distilled white vinegar
3 tablespoons sugar
$\frac{1}{2}$ teaspoon salt
Pinch of turmeric powder
2 shallots, sliced
$\frac{1}{2}$ inch ginger root, julienned
1 clove garlic, peeled and shredded
2 tablespoons raisins

Cut the cucumbers in half lengthwise and remove the seeds. Cut into matchstick pieces $1\frac{1}{2}$ inches in length. Peel the carrot and cut the same size as the cucumber. Dry the cucumbers and carrot in the hot sun for 2 hours. Combine the vinegar, sugar, salt and turmeric and bring to a boil. Remove immediately from the heat and allow to cool. Add the

shallots, ginger, garlic and raisins and mix with the cucumbers and carrot. Store in the refrigerator up to 1 month.

MANGO CHUTNEY

2–3 unripe mangoes (1 pound)

Spice Paste:
6 shallots
5 cloves garlic
$\frac{3}{4}$ inch ginger root
3 red chilies
$\frac{1}{2}$ teaspoon white poppy seeds
1 teaspoon cumin seeds
1 teaspoon fennel seeds
1 teaspoon coriander seeds
$\frac{1}{2}$ teaspoon turmeric powder
2 tablespoons oil

Whole Spices:
3 cloves
$2\frac{1}{2}$ inches cinnamon stick
3 star anise
1 cardamom pod, lightly bruised

Dressing:
4 tablespoons sugar
1 teaspoon salt
$\frac{1}{2}$ cup distilled white vinegar
1 heaped tablespoon raisins

Peel the mangoes and cut the flesh into $\frac{1}{2}$-inch dice.

To prepare **spice paste**, chop shallots, garlic, ginger and chilies finely and blend with spice seeds until fine, adding a little oil to keep the blades turning. Heat remaining oil in pan, add the blended ingredients and **whole spices** and cook gently for

20 minutes. Combine **dressing** ingredients and add, together with the mangoes, to the pan. Reduce to low heat and cook for about $\frac{1}{2}$ hour, until mangoes are soft. Can be kept in the refrigerator for 1 month.

Add more sugar ($1\frac{1}{2}$–2 tablespoons) if mango is very sour.

CHILI PEANUTS WITH ANCHOVIES

4 red chilies
1 shallot
1 tablespoon oil
$\frac{1}{2}$ teaspoon salt
1 tablespoon sugar
$\frac{3}{4}$ cup roasted peanuts with skin
1 ounce dried anchovies (*ikan bilis*), heads and
    intestinal tract removed and fried till crisp

Blend the chilies and shallot together. Heat the oil and gently fry the blended mixture with the salt and sugar for 1 minute. Add the peanuts and anchovies. Stir fry for 3 minutes and remove from heat. Keep in a bottle in the refrigerator up to 3 weeks.

MANGO KERABU

1 large ripe mango (1 pound), peeled
4 mint leaves, roughly chopped
4 cilantro leaves, roughly chopped
1 portion Chili Sauce (see following recipe)

Make the Chili Sauce as instructed. Dice the mango and combine with mint, cilantro and the cooled Chili Sauce. Serve immediately.

CHILI SAUCE

5 red chilies, roughly chopped
10 tablespoons water
3 tablespoons sugar
10 tablespoons distilled white vinegar
1 teaspoon salt

Blend chilies with water. Add the remaining ingredients and bring to a boil. Remove from heat and allow to cool.

CHILI GINGER SAUCE

6 red chilies, roughly chopped
$1\frac{1}{4}$ inches ginger root, chopped
4 cloves garlic
10 tablespoons water
2 teaspoons salt
5 tablespoons sugar
5 tablespoons lime juice
1 teaspoon sesame oil

Blend together the chilies, ginger, garlic and water. Season to taste with the salt, sugar, lime juice and sesame oil.

FRIED SHALLOTS

$\frac{1}{2}$ pound shallots
4 cups oil

Soak shallots in salted water for 5 minutes. Peel the skin and slice thinly. Drain the shallots and dry thoroughly on a cloth. Heat oil in wok and fry shallots over moderate heat until golden brown.

Remove, drain and leave until cold. Store in airtight container. Do not add salt or the shallots will soften.

STUFFED CHILI PICKLE

$1/2$ small green unripe papaya or 1 small
    white radish
1 teaspoon salt
8 green beans, slashed lengthwise halfway
    down
5-inch piece cucumber, halved crosswise then
    cut in coarse pieces
16 shallots, pricked all over with a fork
$1/2$ cup cauliflower florets, broken very small
$1/2$ cup coarsely cut cabbage
2 inches ginger root, finely shredded
5 cloves garlic, very thinly sliced
1 teaspoon brown mustard seed
2 heaped tablespoons dried prawns, soaked in
    warm water
6 inches fresh turmeric ($1/4$ cup powder)
2 teaspoons dried shrimp paste
2 tablespoons oil
2 cups distilled white vinegar
$3/4$ cup sugar
1 teaspoon salt
4 green chilies

If using papaya, begin 2–3 days in advance by shredding the peeled papaya as finely as possible. Sprinkle with 1 teaspoon salt, mix well and sun dry until completely dried up. Alternatively, finely shred the white radish, salt and dry for about $1/2$ day in the sun.

When the papaya or radish are almost dry, prepare the beans, cucumber, shallots, cauliflower and cabbage, sprinkle with about 1 teaspoon salt and leave in sun for 2–3 hours. Salt the ginger and garlic and sun dry separately for 2–3 hours.

Blend the mustard seed until fine, add dried prawns and blend until fine, then add turmeric, garlic and shrimp paste and blend, adding a little of the oil if necessary. Heat the remaining oil and fry blended ingredients until fragrant, then mix in vinegar, sugar and salt, stirring until dissolved. Remove from heat.

Choose straight chilies with the stalk still on. Slit each chili lengthwise, leaving $1/4$ inch at both ends still intact. Use a sharp knife to carefully remove the seeds and membrane from inside the chilies. Stuff each chili with a little of the dried papaya, then mix with the prepared vegetables and ginger.

Pack carefully into jars. Pour over the vinegar mix and close tightly. Leave 3 days before serving. Will keep at least 1 month without refrigeration.

POPIAH

The Nonya version of a popular Chinese snack using fresh wrappers is very substantial and suitable as a lunch dish with something sweet and sinful to follow. ☺☺☺

1/4 **cup oil**
3 **eggs**

Filling:

8 **shallots**
8 **cloves garlic**
2 **tablespoons salted soy bean paste**
1 **pound jicama (***bengkuang***), shredded**
2 **hard bean curd cakes, fried and shredded**
1 **teaspoon black soy sauce**
4 **ounces peeled shrimp**
1 **cup shredded cabbage**
4 **ounces green beans, shredded (about 1 cup)**
4 **tablespoons sugar**
2 **teaspoons salt**

For Serving:

20 **large fresh** *popiah* **skins**
Sweet black sauce (*tim cheong***) to taste**
10 **cloves garlic, blended to make garlic paste**
6 **red chilies, blended to a paste**
Long-leafed lettuce
1 **cup bean sprouts, blanched**
1/3 **cup dry roasted peanuts, skinned and coarsely ground**
3 **tablespoons fried shallots (page 42)**

Beat the eggs lightly, grease an omelet pan with 1/2 teaspoon oil and make 3 very thin omelets. When cooked, shred finely and set aside.

To make the **filling**, crush the shallots and garlic together with the salted soy bean paste. Heat 1/4 cup oil and fry until fragrant. Reserve 3 teaspoons of this. Leave the remaining fried paste in the pan and add the jicama. Cook for 5 minutes until softened, then add the fried bean curd and cook until very soft. Season with black soy sauce.

Use 1 teaspoon of the reserved seasoning and put in a separate pan to fry the shrimp until cooked; repeat with the cabbage, then with the beans. Mix into the cooked jicama and add sugar and salt. Leave to cool.

To serve, put all prepared ingredients on the table. Place a *popiah* skin on a flat surface and spread with a little sweet black sauce, garlic paste and chili paste. Place one lettuce leaf on top, put on a spoonful of the cooked filling, a few shrimp, some cabbage, beans, bean sprouts, peanuts and shallots. Fold in the sides, roll up and serve immediately.

Helpful hints: *Popiah* skins are similar to the fresh wrappers used for Filipino *lumpia*. If neither are available, use Chinese pancakes, also known as *mu shu* wrappers.

CURRY PUFFS

A perennial favorite originally created by Indian cooks and enjoyed by every Malaysian. ☺ ☺

Filling:

5 tablespoons oil
1 medium-sized red or brown onion, finely chopped
1½ teaspoons *kurma* powder or chicken curry powder
2 teaspoons meat or chicken curry powder
1 teaspoon chili powder
½ teaspoon turmeric powder
2 cups finely diced, cooked chicken
2 large potatoes, boiled and finely diced
1½ teaspoons sugar
½ teaspoon black pepper
½ teaspoon salt

Pastry:

4 cups white flour
10 tablespoons butter or margarine
Just over ¾ cup water
½ teaspoon salt

Make the **filling** first. Heat oil and fry the onion gently until golden brown. Add the curry powders, chili, turmeric and fry gently. Add the chicken, potatoes, sugar, pepper and salt and cook for 5 minutes. Mix well and leave aside to cool.

To make **pastry**, mix flour with butter or margarine, water and salt and knead well. Let it rest for ½ hour. Cut the dough into circles 3 inches in diameter. Take a tablespoon of filling and place in center. Fold pastry over to make a half circle and crimp at edges. Deep fry in hot oil until golden.

Helpful hints: Not all margarines are suitable for pastry, owing to their high moisture content. The Malaysian brand, Planta, is recommended; Crisco is a suitable substitute. If meat or chicken curry powder is not available, substitute plain curry powder.

KUIH PIE TEE
Top Hats

Delightfully crisp little cases with a vegetable filling are a Nonya teatime treat. With a rim on the cases, they resemble "top hats." ☺☺☺

Top Hat Cases:
1 mold (*see photograph opposite*)
$^3/_4$ cup white flour
$^1/_2$ teaspoon rice flour
1 egg, beaten
1 cup water
A pinch of salt
Oil for deep frying

Top Hat Filling:
1 tablespoon oil
3 cloves garlic, finely chopped
3 ounces peeled shrimp, chopped
   (about 8 large)
1 pound jicama (*bengkuang*), shredded
2 cups shredded carrot
Pepper to taste
$^1/_2$ teaspoon salt
1 teaspoon sugar

Garnish:
Shredded omelet made with 1 beaten egg
Finely chopped spring onion
1 red chili, finely sliced

Make the **cases** first. Put both flours in mixing bowl, add egg, water and salt and mix well. Whisk the batter until smooth and then put through a sieve. Pour into a glass.

Heat oil in saucepan with the mold in the oil. Turn down the heat to medium. Dip mold into batter so that it is thoroughly coated. The mold must not be too hot; the batter should not sizzle when the mold is placed in. Allow the excess batter to dip off and plunge the mold into oil.

To make the batter separate from the mold while frying, start jiggling it lightly up and down as soon as it is placed in the oil. The batter should open and slip away from the mold with slight shaking. Let the case cook until light brown. Store in airtight container.

To make the **filling**, heat the oil in a saucepan and fry the garlic and shrimp until lightly brown. Add the jicama and carrot and season with the pepper, salt and sugar. Cook for 5 minutes.

To serve, put a little of the filling in top hat cases. Garnish and serve with chili sauce.

Helpful hints: It may take a few tries to successfully create the "top hat" cases. It is essential that the oil is the right temperature and that the mold is sufficiently hot so that when it is dipped into the glass of batter, the batter clings to the mold until the batter-covered mold is put back into the hot oil. If you cannot make the batter form a rim to the "top hat," don't worry; many cooks just make straight-sided cases which are easier to achieve.

SUPERIOR WON TON SOUP

Stuffed ravioli-like dumplings or *won ton* in soup are found in Chinese restaurants throughout the world, but this version is definitely a cut above, thanks to the excellent stock made with dried scallops, chicken and anchovies. ☺☺☺

15 *won ton* skins
6 cups basic stock (*see below*)
1½ cups snow peas, blanched for a few seconds
6 dried black mushroom, soaked, boiled until
    soft, thinly sliced
Salt and pepper

Basic Stock:

3 dried scallops
10 ounces boneless chicken
½ cup very fine dried Chinese anchovies
12 cups water
2 cloves garlic, smashed
½ inch ginger root, sliced
½ teaspoon white peppercorns
3 carrots
7 ribs celery

Filling:

8 ounces shrimp, peeled and deveined
4 ounces boneless chicken or pork
4 ounces water chestnuts, peeled
1½ ounces dried black fungus or
    2 dried mushrooms, soaked
1 tablespoon oyster sauce
½ teaspoon salt

A dash of sesame oil
2 tablespoons sugar
A dash of Chinese wine
1 egg, beaten
2 tablespoons cornstarch
1 tablespoon light soy sauce

Prepare the **stock** first by putting all the ingredients in a pot and bringing to the boil. Remove the scum from the surface, lower heat and simmer, covered, for 2 hours. Strain thoroughly before using.

To make the **filling**, chop the shrimp, chicken, water chestnuts and fungus together with a cleaver until fine. Mix in all other filling ingredients.

Put 1 small spoonful of the filling in the center of a *won ton* wrapper and squeeze the edges together in the center. Repeat until all the filling is used.

Bring the cooked stock to a boil, add the *won ton* and simmer for 3–5 minutes or until they rise to the top. Add the snow peas, mushrooms, salt and pepper and serve immediately.

Helpful hint: If you are unable to find dried scallops (which are very expensive), 1 pound of pork bones can substituted to make the stock.

FRIED KWAY TEOW

Fried Rice-flour Noodles

A great hawker or food stall favorite using fresh rice-flour noodles. ⊘ ⊘

1/2 cup oil
2 cloves garlic, finely chopped
1 whole chicken breast, shredded
6–8 large shrimp, peeled
16–20 mussels
10 ounces dried chilies, soaked and blended
   to a paste
1 pound flat rice-flour noodles (*kway teow*)
1/2 cup chopped garlic chives
2 cups bean sprouts
2 eggs, beaten
Pinch of salt
2 tablespoons black soy sauce
4 tablespoons light soy sauce

Heat the oil in the wok. Sauté the garlic for a few seconds, then add chicken breast, shrimp and mussels. Stir for a few moments, then add 5 tablespoons of the chili paste. Cook for 5 minutes. Add noodles, chives, bean sprouts and eggs, season with salt and soy sauces and stir fry until the noodles are thoroughly heated. Serve immediately.

YEN'S BROWN NOODLES

This version of a Cantonese-style dish, deep-fried coils of crisp, light brown noodles bathed in a delicate but delicious sauce, is named after the chef who created it. Packets of *yee mien* noodles should be available in any Chinese food market. ☉

5 ounces dry brown noodles (*yee mien*)
3 cups mustard greens or spinach
Oil for frying
1 clove garlic, finely chopped
6 ounces peeled shrimp
6 ounces chicken or pork, shredded
3 cups water
2 tablespoons oyster sauce
2 tablespoons light soy sauce
1/2 teaspoon black soy sauce
1/2 teaspoon sesame oil
1/2 teaspoon white pepper
1 heaped tablespoon cornstarch, blended in
   3 tablespoons water
2 eggs, lightly beaten

Put the noodles in a colander, sprinkle with a little cold water and leave aside to soften.

Discard hard ends of the vegetable and cut in 1 1/2-inch lengths. Heat about 2 inches oil in a wok and fry the noodles, a handful at a time, turning over until crisp and golden (about 1 minute). Drain and set aside. Repeat with remaining noodles. Arrange noodles in a large wide bowl or deep serving platter.

Leave about 1 tablespoon of oil in the wok and fry the garlic for a few seconds, then add shrimp and chicken or pork. Stir fry until they are cooked, then add water and all seasonings. Bring to the boil, add vegetables and simmer for a minute. Add the cornstarch mixture and cook, stirring, until the sauce thickens and clears. Pour in the beaten egg, stir and pour over the noodles and serve immediately.

Helpful hints: The noodles should have a firm although not crisp and crunchy texture after cooking. The distinctive flavor of this type of noodle makes this simple-sounding dish well worth sampling.

INDIAN MEE GORENG
Indian Fried Noodles

Although noodles were brought to Malaysia by the Chinese, all other ethnic groups have enthusiastically adapted them to suit their tastes. This version is a dish you certainly couldn't find in India. ☺☺

- **10 dried chilies, soaked in hot water**
- **½ cup oil**
- **1 teaspoon dried shrimp paste**
- **3 cloves garlic, finely chopped**
- **6 ounces large shrimp, peeled and deveined**
- **6 ounces boneless chicken, shredded**
- **12 ounces fresh yellow noodles**
- **2 cups mustard greens**
- **1 cup bean sprouts**
- **2 hard bean curd cakes, deep fried and sliced**
- **3 tablespoons light soy sauce**
- **1 teaspoon salt**
- **1 red chili, sliced**
- **1 green chili, sliced**
- **Sprig of cilantro leaves, roughly chopped**
- **Sprig of Chinese celery leaves, roughly chopped**
- **2 spring onions, sliced**
- **2 tablespoons fried shallots (page 42)**
- **6 small fresh limes, halved**

Blend softened chilies to a paste, adding a little oil if necessary. Keep aside 2 tablespoons of oil and heat the remainder over medium heat, add dried shrimp paste and fry for 1 minute. Add chili paste, reduce heat to low and cook, stirring from time to time, for 30 minutes. Remove from pan.

Heat the 2 tablespoons of oil in a wok. Add garlic, cooked chili paste, shrimp and chicken and fry for 3 minutes. Add noodles and fry over medium heat for 3 minutes. Add mustard greens and bean sprouts. Fry for 2 minutes, then add bean curd and stir fry for 3 minutes. Lastly, add soy sauce and salt mixed together. Stir fry for 1 minute.

Garnish with fresh chilies, cilantro, celery leaf, spring onions, fried shallots and fresh lime and serve immediately.

Helpful hint: Cabbage or spinach can be used instead of mustard greens, if preferred.

LAKSA LEMAK

Noodles in Spicy Coconut-milk Sauce

This Nonya version of Laksa, a spicy noodle dish, comes from Malacca. Although it takes some time to prepare, it is well worth the effort. ⌚⌚

½ cup oil
6 sprigs polygonum (*daun kesum*)
2 wild ginger buds, finely sliced
6 cups water
1½ cups thick coconut milk
1 heaped tablespoon sugar
Salt to taste
1 pound thin fresh yellow noodles, or dried noodles, cooked and drained
1 chicken breast, steamed and shredded
1½ cups bean sprouts, blanched
4 ounces peeled shrimp, steamed (about 10 large)

***Spice Paste*:**

8 red chilies
10 shallots
1 stalk lemongrass
¾ inch galangal
¼ inch fresh turmeric (or ½ teaspoon powder)
½ teaspoon dried shrimp paste

***Garnish*:**

3 sprigs polygonum (*daun kesum*), sliced
1 wild ginger bud, finely sliced
1 cucumber, in matchstick shreds
3 eggs, beaten, made into thin omelets and shredded
2 red chilies, sliced
2 spring onions, finely sliced
6 tablespoons Sambal Belacan (see page 39)
6 small round limes or lemon wedges

Chop and blend all the **spice paste** ingredients finely, adding a little of the oil if necessary to keep the blades turning. Heat remaining oil and gently fry the blended ingredients for 10 minutes, stirring from time to time. Add the polygonum, ginger buds and water and bring to a boil. Add thick coconut milk, sugar and salt. Reduce heat and simmer very gently, uncovered, for 10–15 minutes.

To serve, plunge noodles in boiling water for a few seconds, to heat through. Divide the noodles, chicken, bean sprouts and shrimp among 6 individual noodle bowls and top with the sliced polygonum and ginger bud. Pour sauce on top and add a little cucumber, omelet, chilies and spring onion. Serve with the Sambal Belacan and cut limes in a separate dish.

***Helpful hints*:** The sauce can be prepared in advance, and the garnishing ingredients readied although not sliced to ensure maximum fragrance and freshness. If fresh noodles are not available, use dried rice vermicelli (*meehoon*) or any dried Chinese wheat-flour noodles.

ASAM LAKSA PENANG
Sour Penang Noodle Soup

There are two definite groups within Malaysia: those whose favorite is Laksa Lemak, a spicy noodle soup bathed in coconut milk sauce, and those who prefer the sour, fragrant Penang version, which has a pronounced fishy flavor. Try both and see which group you fall into. ① ① ①

1¼ pounds small Chubb mackerel
   (*ikan kembong*)
6 cups water
5 tablespoons tamarind pulp, soaked and
   squeezed for juice
2 wild ginger buds, sliced
3 sprigs polygonum (*daun kesum*), sliced
½–1 tablespoon sugar, to taste
1¼ pounds fresh coarse rice noodles (*laksa*)

Spice Paste:

5 shallots
2 stalks lemongrass
1 inch fresh turmeric (or 2 teaspoons powder)
3 dried red chilies, soaked in warm water
6 fresh red chilies
1 teaspoon dried shrimp paste

Garnish:

1 cucumber, peeled and shredded
6 sprigs polygonum (*daun kesum*), sliced
Few sprigs mint, torn
3 large red onions, sliced
3 red chilies, sliced
½ fresh pineapple, cut in shreds
Small bowl of black prawn paste (*hay koh*),
   diluted in a little warm water

Simmer the cleaned whole fish in water until cooked. Remove fish, cool, and remove the flesh from the bones. Break up the flesh. Strain the stock carefully and return to a large pan with the fish, tamarind juice, ginger buds, polygonum and sugar.

Blend the **spice paste** ingredients finely and add to the fish stock. Simmer for 20–30 minutes.

Prepare all garnish ingredients. Blanch the noodles in boiling water, drain and divide among 6 bowls. Pour over the fish stock and garnish the top of each bowl. Allow diners to add the black prawn paste themselves, as the taste is rather pungent.

Helpful hints: If Chubb mackerel is not available, choose another well-flavored fish to ensure the soup has its characteristic fishy taste.

NASI KERABU
Rice with Fresh Herbs

The wonderfully fragrant herbs normally found in a kitchen garden are combined with rice to make this popular Kelantan dish, traditionally served with Ayam Percik, either Coconut or Beef Serunding and a chili *sambal*. (Rice with lots of fresh herbs is known as Nasi Ulam in other northern states of Peninsular Malaysia.) As many of these herbs do not have a common English name and are not available outside Malaysia, suggested substitutes are given below. 🕐🕐

> 1 cup uncooked rice
> 1¹/₂ cups water
> 2 stalks lemongrass, smashed
> ³/₄ inch galangal, smashed
> 2 screwpine (*pandan*) leaves
> 2 fragrant lime leaves
> 2 tablespoons thick coconut milk
> ¹/₂ teaspoon salt

Accompaniments:
> 2 *daun maduk*
> 1 *cekur* (zedoary) leaf
> 2 fragrant lime leaves
> 1 sprig *daun kemangi* (basil)
> 1 *daun kunyit* (turmeric leaf)
> 1 sprig *daun kesum* (polygonum)
> 1 stalk *daun renganga*
> 3 *daun salam*
> 1 sprig *daun selum*

> 1 stalk lemongrass
> 1 shallot
> 1 *bunga kantan* (wild ginger bud)
> 1 cucumber

Wash the rice well and place in a rice cooker or pan together with the water, lemongrass, galangal, screwpine leaves, fragrant lime leaves, coconut milk and salt. Bring to a boil and cook, stirring once or twice.

Slice all the **accompaniment** ingredients very finely and arrange on a large platter. Pile the cooked rice in the center and allow each diner to mix through the herbs according to taste. Serve with Coconut Serunding (page 104) and Ayam Percik (page 90).

Helpful hints: Alternative herbs and accompaniments include raw green beans, any type of basil, pennywort or *kottu kala* (known in Malaysia as *daun pegaga*), cilantro leaf, nasturtium leaf, mint, watercress, celery leaves, cabbage or lettuce, etc. In some Malaysian markets, bundles of mixed herbs are sold under the name *ulam* for use in this dish.

NAŞI BOKHARI
Spicy Rice with Chicken

Arab and Indian influences are evident in this richly flavored rice, similar to a *pilau* or *biryani*. It is particularly popular in the northeastern states of Peninsular Malaysia. ☺☺☺

½ chicken, cut into serving pieces
2 tablespoons tomato paste
½ cup evaporated milk
1 tablespoon lime juice
3 tablespoons fried shallots (page 42)
Salt to taste
3 tablespoons ghee
2 cups long-grain rice (preferably *basmati*)

Spice Paste for Marinade:

3 tablespoons coriander seeds
2 tablespoons fennel seeds
1 tablespoon cumin seeds
¾ inch cinnamon stick
2 cloves
2 cardamom pods, husk discarded
2 star anise
1 teaspoon black peppercorns
1 teaspoon turmeric powder
1 teaspoon white poppy seeds (optional)
5 shallots
2 cloves garlic
¾ inch ginger root
6 almonds
½ cup water

Spice Paste for Rice:

2 shallots
2 cloves garlic
1 inch ginger root
1 tablespoon ghee
¾ inch cinnamon stick
1 clove
1 star anise
1 cardamom pod
2 tablespoons evaporated milk

Garnish:

½ cup raisins
3 tablespoons fried shallots (page 42)
1 tablespoon roasted flaked almonds

Grind dry spices first, then grind remaining **marinade spice paste** ingredients and combine. Marinate chicken with the spices, tomato paste, milk, lime juice, shallots and salt and refrigerate overnight.

Heat ghee in a saucepan and fry chicken over low heat, adding water if it threatens to burn. Sauté for ½ hour or until the chicken is cooked. Separate the chicken from the gravy and set chicken aside.

To cook the **rice**, purée the shallots, garlic, ginger and ¼ cup water. Sauté in ghee and add the remaining spices, chicken gravy and milk. Add the rice and cook until brown, stirring occasionally. When the rice is dried and cooked, add raisins, fried shallots, almonds and chicken and stir well.

ROTI JALA AND SAMBAL UDANG
Lacy Pancakes and Shrimp Sambal

ROTI JALA

These lovely lacy pancakes are an ideal accompaniment to any dish with lots of rich gravy and are particularly popular during the Muslim fasting month and on special occasions. ☻☻

- 4 cups white flour
- 2 cups fresh milk
- 2 eggs
- 1 teaspoon salt
- ½ teaspoon turmeric powder
- 1 tablespoon oil
- 1 tablespoon ghee or butter

Sift the flour into a large bowl. Beat the milk and eggs together and mix with the flour, salt and turmeric. Stir until the batter becomes smooth, then put through a sieve. Add oil and set aside.

Heat a nonstick pan and brush surface with ghee or butter. Pour a ladleful of batter into a special Roti Jala funnel or substitute (see below) and make quick circular movements over the pan to form a lacy pattern. When the pancake is cooked, remove and fold into a triangular shape. Repeat the method until all the batter is finished.

Helpful hints: The Roti Jala funnel is a cup with four spouts; an alternative is a plastic squeeze bottle with a reasonably wide hole.

SAMBAL UDANG

This piquant Malay shrimp dish is a firm favorite throughout the country. Take care not to overcook the shrimp or they will become tough. ☻☻

- ½ cup oil
- 2 tablespoons brown sugar
- 1 teaspoon salt
- 3 tablespoons thick coconut milk
- 4 tablespoons lime juice
- 1 pound medium-sized shrimp, peeled and deveined

Spice Paste:
- 10 red chilies
- 3 medium-sized red onions
- 1 inch galangal
- 10 cloves garlic
- 3 candlenuts

Chop all the **spice paste** ingredients, then blend until fine, adding a little of the oil if necessary to keep the blades turning.

Heat oil in a saucepan and fry the blended ingredients for about 10 minutes until fragrant. Add brown sugar, salt and coconut milk and bring to a boil. Add lime juice and shrimp and simmer for 5 minutes or until the shrimp are cooked.

SAMBAL TERONG & NASI KEMULI

Eggplant with Basil & Nonya Wedding Rice

SAMBAL TERONG

This Nonya recipe, using the small Asian eggplants, adds basil for extra flavour. ☉

1 pound small eggplants
2 cups oil
$\frac{1}{2}$ cup basil sprigs
salt and sugar to taste

Spice Paste:
3 red chilies
5 shallots
4 cloves garlic
1 teaspoon dried prawns, soaked
1 tablespoon salted soy bean paste

Opposite:
Sambal Terong
(left) and Nasi
Kemuli (right).

Wash the eggplants but do not peel. Halve length-wise and cut into $1\frac{1}{2}$-inch pieces. Chop and blend the **spice paste** ingredients finely and set aside.

Reserve 4 tablespoons oil and heat the rest in a wok. When the oil is very hot, deep fry the eggplant pieces until brown. Drain and set aside. Drain out the oil, wipe the wok and add the reserved oil. Gently fry the blended ingredients for 5 minutes, then add the fried eggplants, basil, salt and sugar. Cook, stirring frequently, for 2–3 minutes, then serve.

NASI KEMULI

Simple but tasty, Nasi Kemuli is a must at Nonya weddings. ☉

1 cup coriander seeds
2 inches cinnamon stick
2 whole star anise
2 cloves
1 cardamom pod
4 cups water
1 tablespoon ghee
$1\frac{1}{2}$ cups long-grain rice, washed and drained
1 teaspoon dark soy sauce
1 teaspoon salt
2 tablespoons raisins

Spice Paste:
3 shallots
$\frac{1}{2}$ inch ginger root
2 cloves garlic

Combine all the whole spices with water and simmer, uncovered, until the liquid is reduced to 2 cups.

Pound or blend the **spice paste**, then gently fry in the ghee. Remove from the heat and add rice, soy sauce and salt. Mix well and add the 2 cups of liquid together with all the whole spices. Stir well, cover and cook until the rice is done. Add the raisins just before serving.

ROTI CANAI
Flaky Fried Indian Bread

A really good Roti Canai is feather-light, crisp, non-greasy and, some would say, the Indian community's greatest culinary contribution to Malaysia. Roti Canai is a much lighter, flakier version of an Indian bread known as Roti Paratha. ⏲ ⏲

8 cups white plain flour
2 eggs, beaten
1 teaspoon salt
2–3 tablespoons sugar
7 tablespoons butter or ghee, melted
2 cups water
2 tablespoons condensed milk
½ cup ghee or oil for frying

Sift flour into a mixing bowl, add eggs, salt, sugar and melted butter. Combine water with the condensed milk and add to the mixture. Mix well to make a soft dough. Roll dough into a ball and cover with a damp cloth. Leave to rest in a warm place for 30 minutes.

Divide dough into 12 small balls. Coat in ghee or oil, cover and leave to rest for a minimum of 20 minutes or up to 4 hours.

Heat an iron griddle or heavy pan, and coat with oil. Flatten dough balls and stretch out as far as possible. Fold edges inward, continue until you have a round shape 6 inches in diameter. This is required to give the bread a layered texture. Fry the *roti* individually until crisp and golden, adding more ghee or oil as necessary.

Helpful hint: It takes great skill to swing out the dough in circles to stretch it paper thin, as the "Roti man" does with a theatrical flourish. Most home cooks use the bottom of a very large cooking pan and with oiled hands, slowly stretch and push the dough out.

NONYA SHRIMP SALAD

Contrasting flavors and textures bring excitement to this combination of vegetables, shrimp, sweet sauce, herbs and crunchy shrimp crackers. It makes a delicious starter to any meal. ☺☺

1 head long-leaf or Romaine lettuce, torn in long shreds
2 small carrots, cut in matchsticks
2 small white radishes, cut in matchsticks
2 small cucumbers, halved lengthwise, seeded and sliced
1 starfruit, halved lengthwise and sliced (optional)
3 tomatoes, cut in wedges
1 pound shrimp, steamed and peeled

Dressing:
15 red chilies
6–8 cloves garlic
1 cup bottled Chinese plum sauce
1 cup sweet red sauce or 1 cup light palm sugar syrup
$1/2$ cup lime juice
2 tablespoons light soy sauce
1 tablespoon sesame oil
$1/2$ cup peanuts, fried, skins removed and coarsely ground

Garnish:
Deep-fried prawn crackers
Fresh cilantro
Fried shallots (page 42)

To make **dressing**, put chilies and garlic in blender and grind, adding a little of the plum sauce to keep blades turning. When finely ground, add rest of dressing ingredients, except peanuts, blend just to combine and set aside. Add the peanuts only just before serving.

Prepare all remaining ingredients. Divide among 6 plates, starting with the lettuce and finishing with the shrimp. Pour on the dressing and top with garnish.

Helpful hints: Different brands of plum sauce and sweet red Chinese sauce vary in their sugar content, so take care to adjust the dressing to your taste. If using palm sugar syrup, boil 1 cup palm sugar with $1\frac{1}{2}$ cups water until dissolved.

NANAS LEMAK & IKAN ASAM PEDAS

Pineapple and Shrimp Curry & Hot Sour Fish Curry

NANAS LEMAK

Pineapples are a perfect partner to fish and shrimp, as this piquant curry proves. ☻☻

½ fresh just-ripe pineapple
2 cups water
4 tablespoons oil
8 ounces medium-sized shrimp, peeled and deveined
1½ cups thick coconut milk
Salt to taste

Spice Paste:

6 red chilies
8 shallots
2 stalks lemongrass
½ teaspoon dried shrimp paste
½ teaspoon turmeric powder
2 cloves garlic

Opposite:
Nanas Lemak (left) and Ikan Asam Pedas (right) shown here with Dried Cucumber Acar. Recipe for Dried Cucumber Acar is on page 40.

Peel the pineapple, remove the eyes and cut lengthwise into quarters. Remove core, wash and cut into small triangular pieces.

Blend **spice paste** ingredients with ½ cup water. Heat oil in a saucepan and fry the blended ingredients for 5 minutes. Add pineapple, stir fry for another 5 minutes, then add remaining 1½ cups water. When pineapple is soft, add the shrimp, coconut milk and salt. Stir well, lower heat and simmer, uncovered, for 10 minutes.

IKAN ASAM PEDAS

Fragrant and spicy, this curry is enriched by a touch of coconut milk. ☻☻

⅓ cup oil
½ inch galangal, smashed
2 slices *asam gelugur*, or 1 heaped tablespoon tamarind pulp, soaked in water for juice
2½ cups water
6 thick fish fillets or cutlets
4 sprigs polygonum (*daun kesum*), chopped
Salt to taste
1 teaspoon sugar
3 tablespoons thick coconut milk

Spice Paste:

15 dried chilies, soaked in hot water
2 candlenuts
4 cloves garlic
10 shallots
½ teaspoon turmeric powder
1 cup water

Chop and blend **spice paste** ingredients finely. Heat oil in a saucepan, then fry the galangal and blended ingredients for 5 minutes. Add the *asam gelugur* or tamarind pulp. Add ½ cup of water and cook for another 5 minutes. Add the rest of the water and bring to a boil. Add the fish, polygonum, salt, sugar and coconut milk and simmer, uncovered, for another 5 minutes.

SPICY SHRIMP IN A SARONG

A "sarong" of fragrant screwpine or banana leaf adds both a decorative touch and a subtle fragrance to the shrimp; it can, however, be omitted if not available. ⏱ ⏱

1 pound large shrimp, shelled and deveined
Salt and pepper to taste
1 tablespoon lime juice
$1/2$ cup thick coconut milk
1 tablespoon palm sugar syrup (*see helpful hint*)
***Pandan* leaves or $1^1/_2$-inch-wide strips of banana leaf**

Spice Paste:

8 shallots
5 cloves garlic
2 candlenuts
$^3/_4$ inch galangal
6 red chilies
1 teaspooon turmeric powder
1 teaspoon dried shrimp paste

Opposite:
Spicy Shrimp in a Sarong shown here with Nasi Bokhari. Recipe for Nasi Bokhari is on page 64.

Season the shrimp with salt, pepper and lime juice. Chop and blend the **spice paste** ingredients until fine. Combine the blended ingredients, coconut milk, palm sugar syrup and shrimp. Marinate for 4–6 hours.

Wrap the center of each shrimp with a screwpine leaf or strip of banana leaf and secure with a toothpick. Barbecue over very hot charcoal or cook under a grill for about 2–3 minutes on each side, taking care not to overcook.

Helpful hint: Make palm sugar syrup by simmering $1/2$ tablespoon chopped palm sugar in 2 tablespoons water until liquid is reduced by half.

BUTTER SHRIMP & BLACK PEPPER CRAB

BUTTER SHRIMP

A relatively recent Malaysian creation, this combines traditionally Malay, Chinese, Indian and Western ingredients. ☻☻

1$\frac{1}{4}$ pounds large shrimp
Oil for deep frying
2–3 tablespoons butter
15 bird's-eye chilies, roughly chopped
10–15 sprigs curry leaves
2 cloves garlic, finely chopped
$\frac{1}{2}$ teaspoon salt
2 tablespoons sugar
$\frac{1}{2}$ teaspoon light soy sauce
$\frac{1}{2}$ teaspoon Chinese wine
$\frac{1}{2}$ grated coconut, dry fried until golden

Opposite:
Butter Shrimp (top left) and Black Pepper Crab (bottom right).

Remove heads from the shrimp but leave on shells. Slit down the back to remove intestinal tract, trim feelers and legs and dry shrimp thoroughly. Heat the oil and deep fry the shrimp. Drain and reserve.

Melt the butter, add chilies, curry leaves, garlic and salt and fry for 2 minutes. Add shrimp, sugar, soy sauce, wine and grated coconut. Cook over high heat for 1–2 minutes, stirring frequently. Serve immediately.

Helpful hint: Do not use frozen shrimp as the texture after thawing is not suitable for this recipe.

BLACK PEPPER CRAB

This is a real Malaysian dish, starting with mud crabs and Chinese seasonings, adding Indian black pepper and curry leaves, enriching the flavor with butter and then tossing in Malay bird's-eye chilies for a knock-out result. ☻☻

3 fresh mud crabs or soft-shell crabs
    (about 1 pound each)
Oil for deep frying
2 tablespoons butter
2 shallots, thinly sliced
2 cloves garlic, very finely chopped
1 tablespoon salted soy beans, mashed
2 tablespoons dried prawns, roasted and
    ground
2 tablespoons black pepper, ground coarsely
$\frac{1}{2}$ cup curry leaves
10 red or green bird's-eye chilies, chopped
2 tablespoons black soy sauce
3 tablespoons sugar
2 tablespoons oyster sauce

Clean the crabs and cut in half, discarding the spongy "dead man's fingers." Smash the claws with a cleaver to allow the seasonings in. Deep fry the crabs until half cooked, drain and set aside.

Heat a wok, melt butter and put in shallots, garlic, salted soy beans, dried prawns, black pepper, curry leaves and chilies. Sauté until fragrant, then add crab and the remaining ingredients. Cook for 5–10 minutes until the crab is done.

INDIAN FISH CURRY

Many Indian fish curries include eggplant and okra, vegetables which seem to have a particular affinity with spices and fish. ☺ ☺

3/4 cup oil
1/2 teaspoon fenugreek seeds
3 pieces of cinnamon stick, each
    3/4 inch long
5 cardamom pods, bruised
7 dried chilies, left wholed
9 shallots, sliced
4 large onions sliced
8 cloves garlic, sliced
1 inch ginger root, sliced
10 tablespoons fish curry powder
1 tablespoon chili powder
1 1/2 teaspoons turmeric powder
1/2 cup tamarind pulp
6 cups water
2 small eggplants, halved lengthwise, then
    cut in 3 and deep fried
7 small okra (ladies' fingers), stalks and tips
    discarded
1 large tomato, cut into 6 wedges
2 sprigs curry leaves
Oil for frying
6 fish fillets, 8 ounces each, seasoned
    with salt and turmeric powder
3 tablespoons sugar
3 teaspoons salt

Opposite:
Indian Fish Curry
shown here with
ghee rice (top left).

Heat oil in a saucepan, and fry fenugreek, cinnamon and cardamom for 2 minutes. Add dried chilies, shallots, onions, garlic and ginger and fry for about 10 minutes, until golden brown and fragrant. Add the curry, chili, and turmeric powders and continue to stir fry for about 3 minutes, until the oil separates from the mixture.

Add 1 cup of the water to the tamarind, squeeze and strain to obtain the juice. Stir into the saucepan and add the remaining water. Bring to a boil and add the deep-fried eggplants, okra, tomato and the curry leaves. Bring to a boil and simmer for 10 minutes.

Heat oil and quickly deep fry the fish until golden. Drain, then add to the curry and simmer for 5 minutes. Add sugar and salt and serve immediately.

Helpful hints: The curry sauce and vegetables can be cooked in advance, and the fish fried and set aside. Combine the two and simmer just before serving. Substitute regular curry powder if fish curry powder is unavailable.

SALTED FISH AND PINEAPPLE CURRY

Salted fish is popular in Malaysia, and not just as a standby for times when fresh fish may be unavailable owing to monsoon storms. This Eurasian curry uses good quality dried fish cut in $\frac{1}{2}$-inch-thick slices. ☺☺

1 just-ripe pineapple
4 ounces salted fish, cut in large cubes
$\frac{1}{4}$ cup oil
$\frac{1}{2}$ cup water
$1\frac{1}{2}$ cups thick coconut milk
Salt to taste

Spice Paste:

6 shallots
3 red chilies
1 inch fresh turmeric (or 2 teaspoons powder)
1 inch galangal
2 stalks lemongrass
$\frac{1}{2}$ teaspoon dried shrimp paste
$\frac{1}{2}$ teaspoon salt

Peel the pineapple, clean and quarter, remove cores, wash and cut into triangular pieces. Blend half the pineapple with about $\frac{1}{4}$ cup water to make a purée and set aside.

Soak the fish in water for about 10 minutes, then drain and dry well.

Chop **spice paste** ingredients, then blend until fine. Heat the oil in a saucepan, add the blended spice paste and stir fry gently for 5 minutes. Add pineapple cubes and stir fry until well coated with spices. Add the salted fish, the pineapple purée, water and coconut milk. Reduce heat and simmer gently for about 10–15 minutes, until pineapple is tender. Add salt to taste.

Helpful hints: Blending half the pineapple gives a lovely sweet flavor to the curry sauce. You can substitute shrimp for the salted fish.

BORNEO FISH & SABAH VEGETABLE

BORNEO MARINATED FISH

Spanking fresh fish marinated with lemon juice and spiced up with lashings of ginger, shallots and chilies is a favorite among Sarawak's Melanau people, who call their version Umai, and Sabah's Kadazans, who call it Hinava. ☺☺☺

**1 pound very fresh white fish
(Spanish mackerel preferred)**
¹⁄₃ cup freshly squeezed lime or lemon juice
2–3 red chilies
1 teaspoon salt
6–8 shallots, thinly sliced
2 inches ginger root, very finely shredded
2 sprigs fresh cilantro leaves, roughly chopped
2 sprigs Chinese celery, roughly chopped

*Opposite:
Borneo Fish (left)
and Sabah
Vegetable (right).*

Remove all skin and bones from the fish and cut it in thin slices. Keep aside 2 tablespoons of lime juice, then soak the fish in the remaining juice for at least 30 minutes, stirring once or twice, until the fish turns white. Drain and discard lime juice.

While the fish is marinating, pound the chilies with salt until fine. When fish is ready, mix it with the chilies, shallots, ginger, fresh herbs and reserved lime juice. Taste and add more salt if desired. Serve immediately as part of a rice-based meal.

SABAH VEGETABLE

Cekuk manis (*Sauropus albicans*), a shrub with edible leaves, grows wild throughout Southeast Asia. A vegetable grower in Lahad Datu, Sabah, discovered a method to make it grow quickly so that the stems are edible, earning it the name Sabah vegetable or even Sabah asparagus. Any leafy green vegetable can be cooked in this way. ☺

¹⁄₂ pound Sabah vegetable or leafy greens
¹⁄₂ teaspoon dried shrimp paste
2 red chilies
2 shallots
1 clove garlic
1 tablespoon oil
Salt to taste

Pinch off any tough stems at the the end of the Sabah vegetable and cut in 2-inch lengths. Alternatively, wash, dry and coarsely chop leafy greens such as water spinach (*kangkung*) or regular spinach.

Pound or blend shrimp paste, chopped chilies, sliced shallots and garlic until coarse. Heat oil in a wok and fry the pounded mixture for 2–3 minutes, then add vegetables and stir fry quickly until just cooked. Add salt to taste and serve.

PORTUGUESE BAKED FISH

Despite the name, there's nothing Iberian about this well-known fish creation from Malacca's Portuguese Settlement, which blends Malay spices and herbs with Chinese soy sauce for a unique taste. ☺ ☺

2 teaspoons chili powder
5 fragrant lime leaves, very finely sliced
$\frac{3}{4}$ cup oil
1 teaspoon sesame oil
$\frac{1}{4}$ teaspoon soy sauce
$\frac{1}{2}$ teaspoon salt
$\frac{1}{4}$ teaspoon sugar
Banana leaf
Aluminum foil
1 whole fish, weighing about $1\frac{1}{2}$ pounds or
    6 white fish fillets

Spice Paste:

3 onions
6 red chilies
1 scant teaspoon dried shrimp paste
$\frac{1}{2}$ inch galangal
2 stalks lemongrass
5 candlenuts
1 cup water

Chop **spice paste** ingredients, then blend finely with the water. Mix in the chili powder and lime leaves, then fry gently in the oil for about 5 minutes. Combine with the sesame oil, soy sauce, salt and sugar. Mix well and leave to cool.

Cut a large rectangle of banana leaf and brush with oil. If using a whole fish, remove scales, gills and stomach. Cut down the underneath side of the fish from the tail to head and flatten fish with your hand. Slash down either side of the backbone from head to tail, to release the fish flesh from the bones and allow the spice paste to penetrate. Rub the cooked spice paste all over the fish, pushing it well into the slits. If using fish fillets, coat generously on either side with the paste.

Fold the fish in a package in banana leaf and wrap again in foil to secure it. If using fillets, wrap each individually and fasten with a toothpick. Bake, grill or barbecue until cooked.

Helpful hint: The spice paste can be prepared several hours in advance, and rubbed into the fish just before cooking.

SATE AYAM

Chicken Satay & Satay Sauce

The tantalizing aroma of seasoned meat or chicken cooking over a charcoal fire, annointed from time to time with oil spread with a "brush" of fragrant lemongrass, is irresistible. No wonder this Malay dish is Malaysia's all-time favorite. ☺☺☺

2 chicken legs and thighs, deboned and cut
    into serving pieces
$^1\!/_2$ teaspoon chili powder
3 tablespoons sugar
$^1\!/_2$ teaspoon salt
1 teaspoon turmeric powder
Skewers
Oil
1 stalk lemongrass, lightly bruised

Spice Paste:
    6 shallots
    3 stalks lemongrass
    1 clove garlic
    1 tablespoon coriander seeds
    2 tablespoons oil

Opposite:
Chicken Satay (above) shown here with Ketupat (below).

Chop the **spice paste** ingredients and blend together with the oil until fine. Combine blended paste with the chicken, chili powder, sugar, salt and turmeric powder and marinate for 12 hours.

Thread 4–5 pieces of meat onto each skewer. Grill over a charcoal fire, constantly brushing with crushed lemongrass dipped in oil. Turn frequently to prevent burning. Meat should be slightly blackened on the outside and just cooked inside.

Serve with satay sauce, sliced cucumber, sliced raw onion and compressed rice cakes.

SATAY SAUCE

2 cups dry roasted peanuts, skinned
$^1\!/_3$ cup oil
1 heaped tablespoon tamarind pulp, soaked in
    4 tablespoons water
1 cup water
1 tablespoon sugar
Salt to taste

Spice Paste:
    6–8 dried chilies, soaked in hot water
    6 cloves garlic
    3 shallots
    4 stalks lemongrass
    1 inch galangal
    2 tablespoons coriander seeds
    1 teaspoon cumin seeds

Crush the peanuts coarsely and set aside.

Chop the **spice paste** ingredients and blend until fine. Heat oil and fry spice paste together with tamarind pulp until fragrant, adding the water a little at a time. Add sugar, salt and peanuts. Mix thoroughly and set aside. Serve at room temperature with satay.

AYAM PERCIK

Spicy Barbecued Chicken

It's not surprising that this beautifully seasoned chicken, barbecued over a charcoal fire, is so popular, sold at roadside food stalls and markets all over the northeastern state of Kelantan. ☺ ☺ ☺

5 whole chicken legs
4 tablespoons cooking oil
1 slice *asam gelugur* or 2 teaspoons tamarind pulp
4 stalks lemongrass, bruised
1 cup water
1 cup thick coconut milk
1½ tablespoons sugar
Salt to taste

Marinade:

1 teaspoon turmeric powder
1 teaspoon chili powder
1 tablespoon sugar
½ teaspoon salt

Opposite:
Ayam Percik shown here with Nasi Kerabu. Recipe for Nasi Kerabu is on page 62.

Spice Paste:

3 red chilies
6 cloves garlic
5 shallots
4 candlenuts
¾ inch ginger root
9 dried chilies, soaked in hot water

Mix the **marinade**, combine with the chicken and set aside for 1 hour.

Chop the **spice paste** ingredients and blend finely. Heat oil in a saucepan and fry the spice paste, tamarind and lemongrass for 5 minutes. Add water and cook another 3 minutes. Put in coconut milk, sugar and salt and simmer over medium heat for 5 minutes.

Barbecue the chicken over a low charcoal fire or under a broiler, basting frequently with the sauce, until the chicken is cooked.

SPECIAL FRIED RICE & CHICKEN WINGS

SPECIAL FRIED RICE

There must be hundreds of versions of fried rice in Malaysia. This one, from a Nonya kitchen, gets its distinctive flavor from the tiny dried salted fish used by Chinese cooks. Smaller than the usual Malay *ikan bilis*, they are sometimes called silverfish in English. ⏱⏱

Opposite:
Barbecued
Chicken Wings
(left) and Special
Fried Rice (right).

4 cups cold cooked rice
$\frac{1}{2}$ cup very small dried anchovies
$\frac{1}{3}$ cup oil
1 clove garlic, finely chopped
6 ounces chicken breast, diced
6 ounces peeled shrimp
3 eggs, beaten
1 tablespoon light soy sauce
Salt and pepper to taste
$\frac{1}{4}$ teaspoon sesame oil
$1\frac{1}{2}$ cups bean sprouts
2 spring onions, finely sliced

Break up the rice with a fork and set aside. Heat enough oil to fry the dried anchovies until crisp. Drain and keep aside. Discard oil.

Heat $\frac{1}{3}$ cup oil and gently fry the garlic for a few seconds, then add chicken and shrimp and stir fry for 3–4 minutes. Raise heat and add egg, stirring until set. Add rice and continue cooking over maximum heat, stirring constantly, until rice is heated through. Add seasonings, bean sprouts and spring onions, stir well, add anchovies and stir again. Serve immediately.

Helpful hint: Rice left overnight is preferred for any fried rice dish, as it is drier and firmer and will result in a better texture.

BARBECUED CHICKEN WINGS

Although often overlooked in the West, chicken wings are highly regarded in Asia for their slightly gelatinous texture. In Malaysia, you will often find them being barbecued, especially at roadside stalls in the evenings, in a special rack that holds a number of wings at a time. ⏱

6 large chicken wings
$\frac{1}{2}$ teaspoon Chinese wine
$\frac{1}{2}$ teaspoon sesame oil
1 tablespoon light soy sauce
2 tablespoons black soy sauce
2 tablespoons oyster sauce
2 tablespoons honey
Salt and pepper to taste

Combine all the ingredients and marinate the chicken wings for 6 hours. Cook over a barbecue pit or under a grill, turning until cooked and golden brown.

DRY MUTTON CURRY & CHICKEN CURRY

DRY MUTTON CURRY

Mutton is popular with both Indians and Malays, who sometimes substitute it with goat. This is a typical Southern Indian curry, with potatoes adding a pleasant soothing flavor and a contrasting texture. ☺ ☺

> 1 pound boneless lamb or mutton leg, cubed
> 5 cups water
> 4 tablespoons chili powder
> 1 teaspoon turmeric powder
> 4 potatoes, peeled and cubed
> $1/2$ cup oil
> 25 shallots, sliced
> $1/2$ inch ginger root, sliced
> 7 cloves garlic, sliced
> 2 sprigs curry leaves
> 2 teaspoons salt
> 2 teaspoons sugar

Bring the lamb, water, chili and turmeric powder to a boil and simmer for 25 minutes. Add potatoes and continue to cook until they are tender and liquid has reduced by half.

In a separate saucepan, heat oil and fry the shallots, ginger and garlic until golden brown. Drain and add to the lamb with the curry leaves and cook until the sauce thickens. Add salt and sugar to taste.

Opposite:
Dry Mutton Curry (top left) and Chicken Curry (bottom right).

CHICKEN CURRY

The use of cinnamon and star anise gives a robust flavor to this Indian chicken curry. ☺ ☺

> $1/4$ cup ghee
> 10–15 dried chilies, soaked and ground to a paste
> 1 cup meat curry powder
> 5 cinnamon sticks, each about 2 inches long
> 3 star anise
> 1 handful curry leaves
> 10 potatoes, peeled and quartered
> 1 chicken, cut into small pieces
> $2^1/2$ cups coconut milk
> Salt to taste
> 1–2 teaspoons sugar

Spice Paste:

> 15 shallots
> 4 cloves garlic
> 1 inch ginger root

Blend the **spice paste** ingredients until fine. Melt the ghee in a large pot, sauté the blended items, then add chili paste and curry powder, mixed with a little water to make a paste. Continue frying until fragrant, then add cinnamon, star anise, curry leaves and potato. Put in chicken and sauté until the chicken is half cooked. Add coconut milk, season with salt and sugar. Simmer until done.

DEVIL CHICKEN CURRY

The large amount of chilies make the fiery name entirely appropriate for this Eurasian curry, which is similar to Indian Vindaloo with its blending of spices and vinegar. The Malaysian touch is given with fresh lemongrass, galangal and dried shrimp paste. ☼☼

1/4 cup oil
2 onions, quartered
2 inches ginger root, shredded
5 cloves garlic, sliced
2 red chilies, halved lengthwise
1 teaspoon salt
1 teaspoon light soy sauce
4 tablespoons sugar
4 potatoes, peeled and quartered
1/2 chicken, cut into serving pieces
1/2 cup distilled white vinegar
3–4 cups water

Spice Paste:
30 shallots
30 dried chilies, soaked and deseeded
1 1/4 inches fresh turmeric (or 2 1/2 teaspoons powder)
1 inch galangal
2 stalks lemongrass
1 teaspoon brown mustard seeds, soaked in water for 5 minutes

Chop **spice paste** ingredients and blend with a little of the oil until fine. Set aside.

Heat remaining oil and fry the onions, ginger, garlic and chilies for 2 minutes. Drain off the oil and set mixture aside.

Fry the blended ingredients with 4 tablespoons oil for 10 minutes, adding the salt and soy sauce. Add sugar, stir well, then put in the potatoes, chicken, vinegar and water. Simmer, uncovered, until chicken is cooked. Taste and adjust seasonings, adding a little more vinegar for a sourer taste, if desired. Add the reserved fried ingredients, stir well and serve with rice.

Helpful hint: Cut the chilies into pieces before soaking, and discard the seeds—which will fall to the bottom of the bowl—to help reduce the heat.

NASI AYAM

Chicken Rice

Chicken served with rice, chili sauce and cucumber is one of the most popular coffee shop and hawker dishes in Malaysia. The Chinese version normally uses chicken simmered in stock, while this Malay recipe uses roast chicken. 🕐🕐🕐

Opposite:
Nasi Ayam
shown here with
(clockwise) chili
sauce, ginger and
dark soy sauce.

Roast Chicken:
1/2 fresh chicken
3 cloves garlic
4 shallots
2 inches ginger root
3 tablespoons oyster sauce
1 tablespoon black soy sauce
2 tablespoons light soy sauce
1 tablespoon tomato sauce
1 tablespoon chili sauce
1 teaspoon chili powder
1 teaspoon salt

Rice:
2 cups uncooked rice, washed thoroughly
1 inch ginger root
3 cloves garlic
4 tablespoons butter
2 *pandan* leaves
Pinch salt
3 tablespoons fried shallots (page 42)

Chili Sauce:
5 red chilies
4 cloves garlic
1 inch ginger root
3 tablespoons lime juice
1 teaspoon sesame oil
Salt and sugar to taste

Garnish:
1 cucumber, sliced

Prepare the **chicken** well in advance. Prick the chicken with a fork to allow seasonings to penetrate. Blend or pound garlic, shallots and ginger, then mix with all other ingredients and rub into chicken. Marinate 4 hours or overnight, if possible. Roast chicken in a 450°F oven for about 20 minutes. Cut into serving pieces and put on a platter garnished with sliced cucumber.

Wash the **rice**, drain and put in a saucepan or rice cooker. Pound the ginger and garlic together and add to rice together with butter, *pandan* leaves, salt and sufficient water to cook the rice. When the rice is cooked, fluff up with a fork, put in a serving bowl and decorate with fried shallots.

Blend all the **chili sauce** ingredients together until fine.

Serve the rice with the chicken, cucumber and chili sauce, with a bowl of clear chicken soup to accompany it if desired.

AYAM LIMAU PURUT & SAYUR LEMAK
Chicken with Lime Leaf & Vegetables in Coconut Milk

AYAM LIMAU PURUT

The charm of this Nonya curry comes from its aromatic fresh herbs and seasonings. ⊘⊘

½ cup oil
½ chicken, cut in serving pieces
1 slice *asam gelugur* or lime juice to taste
½ cup water
1 cup thick coconut milk
4 fragrant lime leaves
Salt to taste

Spice Paste:

2 medium-sized red or brown onions
8 red chilies
3 cloves garlic
1 stalk lemongrass
1¼ inches galangal
1 teaspoon turmeric powder

Chop and blend the **spice paste** ingredients, adding a little of the oil if necessary to keep the blades turning. Heat oil and fry the blended ingredients for about 5 minutes, until fragrant.

Add the chicken, *asam gelugur* and water and simmer until the chicken is half cooked. Add the coconut milk and lime leaves and simmer, uncovered, until the chicken is tender. Add salt and, if using, lime juice to taste.

SAYUR LEMAK

A Nonya adaptation of Malay-style vegetables simmered in seasoned coconut milk. ⊘⊘

3 tablespoons oil
1½ cups water
1½ cups thick coconut milk
1 carrot, cut in 1½-inch matchsticks
1 small eggplant, cut in 1½-inch matchsticks
3 long beans, cut in 1½-inch lengths
¼ cabbage, coarsely shredded
1 hard bean curd cake, deep fried and quartered
Salt to taste

Spice Paste:

2 red chilies
3 candlenuts
5 shallots
½ teaspoon turmeric powder
½ teaspoon dried shrimp paste
1 teaspoon dried prawns, soaked 5 minutes in warm water

Chop the **spice paste** ingredients and blend finely, adding a little oil if necessary to keep the blades turning. Heat the oil and fry the blended ingredients for 5 minutes, then add the water and coconut milk and bring slowly to a boil.

Add the prepared vegetables, bean curd and salt and simmer, uncovered, until the vegetables are just cooked.

Opposite:
Ayam Limau Purut (left) and Sayur Lemak (right).

RENDANG DAGING

Rich Coconut Beef

No festive occasion is complete without this rich Malay dish where beef is cooked to melting tenderness in a fragrant, coconut gravy. ☺☺☺

1/2 cup oil
1 1/4 inches cinnamon stick
2 cloves
4 star anise
2 cardamom pods
1 pound top round beef, cubed
1 cup thick coconut milk
1 slice *asam gelugur*, or 2 teaspoons dried tamarind pulp soaked in warm water for juice
2 fragrant lime leaves, very finely sliced
1 turmeric leaf, very finely sliced
2 tablespoons *kerisik* (*see below*)
1 1/2 teaspoons sugar
Salt to taste

Spice Paste:

2 shallots
3/4 inch galangal
3 stalks lemongrass
2 cloves garlic
3/4 inch ginger root
10 dried chilies, soaked in hot water

Chop the **spice paste** ingredients, then purée in a blender until fine. Heat the oil, add the spice paste, cinnamon, cloves, star anise and cardamom and fry for 5 minutes.

Add the beef, coconut milk and *asam gelugor* or tamarind juice. Simmer uncovered, stirring frequently, until the meat is almost cooked. Add the lime and turmeric leaves, *kerisik*, sugar and salt. Lower the heat and simmer until the meat is really tender and the gravy has dried up. Approximate cooking time is 1 to 1 1/2 hours.

Helpful hints: To prepare the *kerisik*, roast 3 3/4 cups grated fresh coconut in a slow oven until brown. Alternatively, cook in a dry wok, stirring constantly. Let the coconut cool, then grind finely until the oil comes out.

BEAN SPROUT KERABU & SERUNDING

BEAN SPROUT KERABU

This salad from the northern states of Peninsular Malaysia makes an excellent accompaniment to rich or spicy dishes. ☽☽

> 4 tablespoons freshly grated coconut
> 5 cups bean sprouts
> 4 tablespoons oil
> Salt to taste

Spice Paste:

> 8 red chilies
> 6 shallots
> 2 tablespoons dried prawns, washed and drained
> 3 cloves garlic

Opposite:
*Bean Sprout
Kerabu (left) and
Coconut Serunding
(right).*

Fry the coconut over low heat in a wok, stirring constantly, until golden brown. Set aside to cool.

Blanch the bean sprouts in boiling water for just a few seconds, drain, plunge into cold water and drain again, then set aside.

Chop and purée the **spice paste** ingredients finely. Heat oil in a pan and fry the blended ingredients for 10 minutes, adding a little water if the mixture becomes dry. Season and add the roasted coconut. Fry until the mixture is dried. Allow to cool.

Combine with the bean sprouts and serve.

COCONUT SERUNDING

This is traditionally served with Nasi Kerabu. ☽☽

> 1 fresh coconut, grated
> 8 tablespoons oil
> 1 tablespoon fennel powder
> 2 slices *asam gelugur* or 1 teaspoon lime juice
> Salt to taste
> 1 teaspoon sugar
> 1 turmeric leaf, sliced
> 4 fragrant lime leaves, sliced

Spice Paste:

> 15 dried chilies, soaked in hot water
> 2 stalks lemongrass
> $3/4$ inch galangal
> $1/2$ inch turmeric (or 1 teaspoon powder)
> 3 shallots
> 3 cloves garlic

Chop and blend the **spice paste** ingredients. Roast the grated coconut in the oven until light golden. Heat the oil and fry spice paste together with the fennel powder and *asam gelugur* slices for 5 minutes. Add the salt, sugar, lime juice (if using) and roasted coconut. Fry over low heat until the coconut is crisp and dry. Add the turmeric and fragrant lime leaves and cook for another 3 minutes. Leave to cool before serving.

NEW YEAR SALAD & STIR-FRIED PEAS

NEW YEAR SALAD

A firm family favorite during the New Year's Eve reunion dinner, when many other rich dishes are served. ◷

1 large jicama (*bengkuang*)
1 medium-sized carrot
1 dried squid, about 4 inches long
2 tablespoons oil
2 cloves garlic, finely chopped
5 medium-sized shrimp, peeled and diced
$1/3$ cup chicken stock
White pepper
2 tablespoons light soy sauce
Long-leafed lettuce
Hoisin sauce (optional)

Peel the jicama and carrot and cut both into match-stick pieces. Shred dried squid finely (or buy it already shredded) and soak with boiling water to cover for about 10 minutes. Drain well.

Heat oil in a wok and stir fry the garlic for a few seconds. Add the shrimp and cook until they change color, then add the squid. Mix thoroughly, then add the jicama and carrot and cook until the jicama starts to soften. Add chicken stock and simmer, turning from time to time, until the vegetables are soft. Add soy sauce, mix well and serve at room temperature together with a plate of lettuce leaves. Each dinner puts some of the vegetable inside a leaf

Opposite: Stir-fried Peas (left) and New Year Salad (right).

and rolls it up to eat, adding a smear of *hoisin* sauce if desired.

STIR-FRIED PEAS

Tender sugar snap peas contrast beautifully in color and texture with the white garlic and pink shrimp. ◷

$1/2$ pound sugar snap peas
$1/2$ teaspoon Chinese rice wine
2 tablespoons light soy sauce
$1 1/2$ tablespoons oyster sauce
1 tablespoon oil
8 cloves garlic, skins left on and lightly bruised
4 ounces peeled shrimp (approximately 10 large)
$1/2$ cup water or fresh chicken stock
1 heaped teaspoon cornstarch, blended in a little water
$1/2$ teaspoon salt

Blanch the peas in boiling water for no more than 5 seconds, then drain thoroughly. Mix rice wine, soy sauce and oyster sauce and set aside.

Heat oil until very hot and stir fry garlic for a few seconds, then add the shrimp and fry until they change color. Add the peas and mixed seasonings and stir fry for about half a minute, then add water and bring to a boil. Thicken with cornstarch, add salt and serve.

SNAKE GOURD & SPICY PUMPKIN

SNAKE GOURD

Colors and textures contrast beautifully in this southern Indian dish. ✺

- **1 cup yellow lentils**
- **$1/2$ teaspoon turmeric powder**
- **2 cups water**
- **1 snake gourd**
- **4 shallots, sliced**
- **1 clove garlic, sliced**
- **2 tablespoons oil**
- **1 tablespoon brown mustard seed**
- **1 teaspoon salt**
- **1 sprig curry leaves**
- **2 red chilies, seeds removed, sliced**

Wash lentils thoroughly, combine with turmeric and water and simmer until soft.

While the lentils are cooking, prepare the gourd. For a more decorative appearance, scrape the skin deeply lengthwise with a fork and cut in half lengthwise. Remove the pulpy center and cut across in $1/2$-inch slices. Alternatively, peel the gourd, remove the center and cut in circles $1/2$ inch thick.

Fry the shallots and garlic in oil until soft, then add mustard seeds and cook until they begin to pop. Add cooked lentils, gourd and salt, and cook until tender. Just before removing from heat, add curry leaves and chili. Toss and serve.

Helpful hint: If snake gourd is not available, substitute 1 pound of long beans, or slices of any type of summer squash.

SPICY PUMPKIN

Gourds are very popular among Malaysians of Southern Indian origin, especially sweet-tasting pumpkin, which goes well with spices. ✺

- **$1^1/2$-pound pumpkin, peeled and cut in 1-inch pieces**
- **3 tablespoons oil**
- **1 large onion, finely chopped**
- **1 tablespoon brown mustard seeds**
- **2 sprigs curry leaves**
- **1 tablespoon fish or chicken curry powder**
- **2–3 teaspoons chili powder**
- **$1/2$ teaspoon turmeric powder**
- **2 cups water**
- **1 teaspoon salt**
- **Sugar to taste**

Prepare the pumpkin and set aside. Heat the oil and fry the onion until golden, then add mustard seed and curry leaves and fry until mustard seeds pop. Add the spice powders and fry for 30 seconds, then put in pumpkin and stir for a minute or two, until well coated with spices. Slowly add the water, stirring, then add salt and sugar to taste. Simmer, uncovered, until tender and dry.

PISANG JANTUNG

Banana Bud Salad

BANANA BUD SALAD

No Malaysian with bananas growing in the garden would waste the bud of the banana flower, which is also sold in local markets. It tastes surprisingly similar to artichokes. This version of the popular banana bud salad comes from the Portuguese community in Malacca. ☾☾

1 banana bud
4 ounces shrimp (about 10 large), steamed and peeled
2 tablespoons oil
2 teaspoons finely pounded dried prawns
$\frac{1}{3}$ cup thick coconut milk
$\frac{1}{2}$ teaspoon salt
2-inch piece of cucumber, shredded in matchsticks
6 small sour carambola (*belimbing*), very finely sliced lengthwise
1 fresh red chili, finely sliced
4 shallots, sliced
2 small limes, halved

Spice Paste:
3 fresh red chilies
2 cloves garlic
6 shallots
1 teaspoon dried shrimp paste

Remove the outer red leaves of the banana bud and simmer the heart in lightly salted water for 20 minutes. Drain, cool, then discard any hard portion of the boiled banana bud. Cut in half lengthwise, then cut crosswise in coarse slices. Set aside with the cooked shrimp.

Chop the **spice paste** ingredients and blend with $\frac{1}{2}$ cup water. Fry the dried prawns gently in oil over moderate heat for half a minute, then add the blended ingredients and cook for about 2–3 minutes, until fragrant. Add coconut milk and salt and leave to cool.

To serve, put banana bud in the center of a plate, add cucumber, carambola, chili, shallots and lime. Top with shrimp and pour over the cooled sauce.

Helpful hint: If banana bud is not available, substitute with 8 ounces (2 cups) cooked shredded chicken breast.

SAGO WITH HONEYDEW & GULA MELAKA

SAGO WITH HONEYDEW

Chinese desserts are not commonly served in the home, although elaborate restaurant meals often finish with a refreshing dessert such as this. ⏲ ⏲

$3/4$ cup pearl sago
7 cups water
1 cup coconut milk
1 cup sugar
$1/2$ cup water
$1/2$ honeydew melon

Soak sago with 2 cups water for 30 minutes, then drain. Bring the remaining 5 cups water to a boil and add sago. Cook until transparent. Drain in a sieve and wash under cold running water. Leave aside until cool.

Boil together sugar and $1/2$ cup water to make a syrup and allow to cool.

Peel the honeydew, cut in half and discard seeds. Blend half the honeydew to make juice and cut the other half into small cubes, or make small balls with a melon baller. Mix the sago, coconut milk, honeydew juice, honeydew cubes and sugar syrup to taste. Serve chilled.

GULA MELAKA

Smooth sago with creamy coconut milk and golden-brown palm sugar syrup make this one of Malaysia's best-loved desserts. The name literally means "Malacca Sugar," although palm sugar (also known as *gula merah* or "red sugar") is made throughout the country. ⏲ ⏲

12 cups water
3 *pandan* leaves
10 ounces pearl sago
1 cup thick coconut milk
$1/2$ cup palm sugar, boiled with
  $3/4$ cup water to make syrup

Bring the water to boil with the *pandan* leaves. Meanwhile, wash the sago in a sieve, soak in cold water to cover for 3 minutes and drain. When water is boiling, add the sago and simmer for about 15 minutes until it becomes transparent.

Pour the sago into a sieve and wash under cold running water. Place sago into small molds and refrigerate until set.

To serve, unmold the sago in individual serving dishes. Serve with coconut milk and palm sugar syrup.

AIS KACANG

Shaved Ice with Red Beans

A delicious way to beat the heat, Ais (Ice) Kacang is a mound of shaved ice piled onto a mixture of gelatin, red beans and sweet corn. Add a dollop of brightly colored syrup and a generous splash of evaporated milk and it's a treat that not only the children will enjoy. The following amounts are for each individual serving. ⏱ ⏱

- 1 heaped tablespoon red (*azuki*) beans, boiled until soft
- 1 heaped tablespoon sweet corn kernels
- 1 heaped tablespoon finely diced flavored gelatin or jelly
- 1 heaped tablespoon *cendol* (optional)
- 1 tablespoon chopped peanuts
- 1 teaspoon chopped preserved nutmeg fruit (optional)
- Large bowl of shaved ice
- 1 tablespoon palm sugar syrup
- 1 tablespoon red cordial or colored sugar syrup cooked with a *pandan* leaf
- 2 tablespoons evaporated milk

Measure the beans, corn, jelly, *cendol*, peanuts and nutmeg fruit into a bowl. Top with a cone of shaved ice, then pour over the palm sugar syrup, cordial and milk. Serve immediately.

Helpful hints: Ice must be very finely shaved for this dish; try processing it in a food processor or blender. Make palm sugar syrup by simmering ½ tablespoon chopped palm sugar in 2 tablespoons water until liquid is reduced by half.

NONYA PANCAKE

A Nonya version of the Malay stuffed pancake, Kuih Dadar, is served with a coconut sauce as a teatime treat or snack, rather than a dessert, in Malaysia. ☺ ☺ ☺

Batter:

> 10 *pandan* leaves
> 1 cup water
> 1 cup plus 3 tablespoons white flour
> 1 egg
> Scant $^1/_3$ cup fresh milk
> $^1/_4$ teaspoon salt
> 2 teaspoons melted butter

Filling:

> 2 cups grated coconut
> 1$^1/_2$ cups water
> 3 *pandan* leaves
> $^1/_4$ teaspoon salt
> $^3/_4$ cup palm sugar, chopped

Coconut Sauce:

> $^1/_2$ cup thick coconut milk
> $^1/_2$ cup water
> 3 *pandan* leaves
> 1 teaspoon sugar
> 1 teaspoon cornstarch
> Pinch of salt

Prepare the **batter** by blending the *pandan* leaves with water and straining to obtain the juice. Sift the flour into a bowl and add egg, milk, salt and *pandan* juice. Stir until smooth, adding more water if necessary to obtain a thin consistency. Set aside while preparing the filling and sauce.

Combine all **filling** ingredients in a saucepan and simmer over very low heat, stirring occasionally, for about 45 minutes, until thick and dry. Set aside to cool.

Combine all the **coconut sauce** ingredients in a saucepan and stir continuously over low heat until the sauce thickens and clears. Sieve and serve warm or at room temperature.

Cook the pancakes. Grease a nonstick pan with a little butter and pour in enough batter to make a pancake about 6–8 inches in diameter. Cook gently on both sides and reserve. Repeat until all the batter is used.

To serve, put 2–3 tablespoonfuls of the filling in the center of a pancake. Tuck in the edges and roll up cigar fashion. Serve the pancakes, preferably still warm or at room temperature, with the coconut sauce.

Mail-order Sources of Ingredients

The ingredients used in this book can all be found in markets featuring the foods of Southeast Asia. Many of them can also be found in any well-stocked supermarket. Ingredients not found locally may be available from the mail-order markets listed below.

Anzen Importers
736 NE Union Ave.
Portland, OR 97232
Tel: 503-233-5111

Central Market
40th & Lamar St.
Austin, Texas
Tel: 512-206-1000

Dean & Deluca
560 Broadway
New York, NY 10012
Tel: 800-221-7714 (outside NY);
800-431-1691 (in NY)

Dekalb World Farmers Market
3000 East Ponce De Leon
Decatur, GA 30034
Tel: 404-377-6401

Gourmail, Inc.
816 Newton Road
Berwyn, PA 19312
Tel: 215-296-4620

House of Spices
76-17 Broadway
Jackson Heights
Queens, NY 11373
Tel: 718-507-4900

Kam Man Food Products
200 Canal Street
New York, NY 10013
Tel: 212-755-3566

Nancy's Specialty Market
P.O. Box 327
Wye Mills, MD 21679
Tel: 800-462-6291

Oriental Food Market and Cooking School
2801 Howard St.
Chicago, IL 60645
Tel: 312-274-2826

Oriental Market
502 Pampas Drive
Austin, TX 78752
Tel: 512-453-9058

Pacific Mercantile Company, Inc.
1925 Lawrence St.
Denver, CO 80202
Tel: 303-295-0293

Penn Herbs
603 North 2nd St.
Philadelphia, PA 19123
Tel: 800-523-9971

Rafal Spice Company
2521 Russell
Detroit, MI 48207
Tel: 313-259-6373

Siam Grocery
2745 Broadway
New York, NY 10025
Tel: 212-245-4660

Spice House
1048 N. Old World 3rd St.
Milwaukee, WI
Tel: 414-272-0977

Thailand Food Corp.
4821 N. Broadway St.
Chicago, IL 60640
Tel: 312-728-1199

Uwajimaya
PO Box 3003
Seattle, WA 98114
Tel: 206-624-6248

Vietnam Imports
922 W. Broad Street
Falls Church, VA 22046
Tel: 703-534-9441

Index